CATTL

Herb Wharton, born in t
camp, in south-west Quee.
of twelve to go droving. His maternal grandmother was
from the Kooma tribe; his grandfathers were English
and Irish. He has seen most of Queensland from horseback and has worked as a fencer, horse trainer and rodeo
rider, as well as a meatworker and builder. A trustee of
the Eulo Aboriginal Reserve and a life member of the
Stockman's Hall of Fame, he now devotes his time to
writing.

His poetry, short stories, book reviews and essays appear in journals published here and abroad. In 1993 he
was a member of the Black Writers' tour, "My People",
which travelled to Yarrabah, Cairns and Townsville, and
was writer-in-residence at Narrabundah College, ACT.
His novel *Unbranded*, published in 1992, was highly com-
mended in the David Unaipon Award for Aboriginal and
Torres Strait Islander writers, and has been reprinted.

Also by Herb Wharton

Unbranded

For well over a hundred years white Australian writers have produced novels of pastoralism. But the emphasis, even in Vance Palmer, Katharine Susannah Prichard or Xavier Herbert, has been largely on the heroic exploits of the white male ... *Unbranded* represents a major publishing phenomenon because it presents an Aboriginal viewpoint on the pastoral industry and current race relations ... *Unbranded* is written simply but stylishly by a masterly yarn-teller. It sets new standards for fictionalised Aboriginal life-stories.

Ken Goodwin, review in Outrider

Foreword

A fortunate few others became more famous; thousands more suffered greater injustices. Their stories remain untold. But the lives of these few people are remarkable, not only for their personal histories but for the contribution they and thousands of other unrecorded Aborigines have made to the Australian pastoral industry. They overcame misguided prejudices to get equal wages and to escape the missions. They did not acquire great wealth — but they helped to create it for others. And the wealth of the pastoral industry, like the mining industry, came from unrelinquished ancient Aboriginal tribal lands in the form of huge outback sheep and cattle stations.

In fact, the titled English Vesty mob were granted grazing rights to millions of acres for a token fee. They controlled the beef from birth to slaughter then to the butcher's shop in England. The majority of the labour on their stations was Aboriginal — underpaid, underfed. This led to the historic walk-off on Vesty-owned Wave Hill Station and so was born the modern land rights movement, long before the Mabo judgment.

In the country of my birth in south-west Queensland, many Aborigines were moved to missions. For some it was vital to their very survival, but to others it was a tragedy and an injustice. A few remained camped around the stations to provide a handy supply of slave labour. Lots more became the fringe dwellers of western towns, reared in segregation in the yumbas (Murrie camps). Their demands for equality, education and justice led to equal pay long before I began my working life. And a lifetime before the Wave Hill dispute, with no dole or mission handouts, they became independent. In a quest to decide their own destinies many adapted and embraced the best of both worlds, although many had the worst of both worlds imposed upon them.

Our languages were never forbidden. Like assimilation it was always an option. Oppressed and segregated they were, but never downtrodden. The threat of intervention in their lives from the police or inept bosses was always present — in fact, any white man or woman could lodge a complaint and in this way Aborigines were sent to missions.

"Cheeky black bastard! Hey, we'll send ya to Palm Island" (or other such places) — for a lot of Aborigines, this was the ever-present threat hanging over them.

In the past, white Australian politicians have highlighted the horror of Russian gulags in Siberia; but they remained silent about the practice of sending Aborigines to Palm Island. At least those who went to Siberia were still in their own land; for the many sent to Palm Island from their tribal homelands in the arid inland, it was like being deported to another country surrounded by sea, where they remained under the rule of white masters.

For when British law came to Australia, it meant just that — British law did not mean justice so far as Aborigines were concerned. Before the missions were set up, many Aborigines were murdered by whites, yet it was not recorded as murder. In Aboriginal minds the belief grew that a white person could kill an Aborigine and walk free, but an Aborigine could never kill a white person, whatever extenuating circumstances might exist, and hope to escape British law. In fact, sometimes when whites went out to capture an Aboriginal so-called criminal, they not only shot the "criminal" but other Aborigines who happened to be there as well. In this way, many men, women and children were killed. Justice was not accorded to Aborigines through the British law courts. Many times it was dispatched through the barrels of countless guns.

I felt honoured to be allowed to write the stories of these few Aborigines, whose names are now recorded as part of the history of Australia. I hope those who read this book may learn from the past, try to understand the present, and feel inspired to help plan a better future for all Australians.

Herbert Wharton
Cunnamulla, 1994

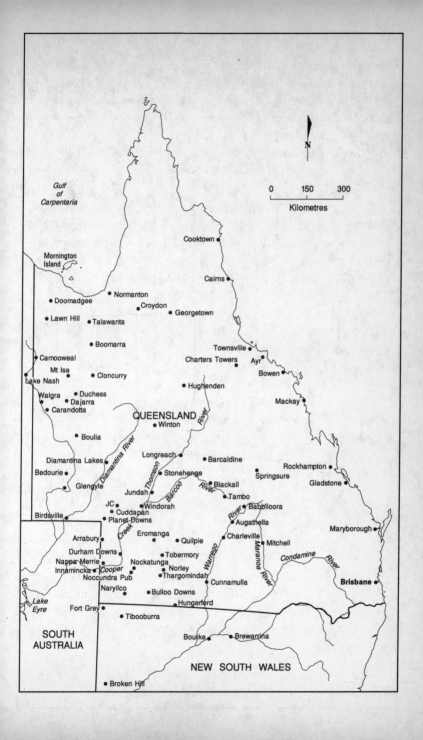

Roy Mahar

A black ball of fluff by the Gil-gi hole

Roy Mahar, like his mother and grandmother, like thousands of generations before them, was born near the Georgina River in far north-west Queensland. Like many Aborigines whose family and tribal life was interrupted by white land rights, Roy told me that all he knew of his father's history was that he had been reared by a white family around Burketown, in Queensland's Gulf country. Roy believes that is how he came to be called "Mahar".

Today, white Australians spend a fortune trying to trace their family history; before the coming of the Europeans, any Aborigine was able to find out about his family relationships simply by asking the elders. In a very short space of time he could be told everything about his ancestry, stretching back to the Dreamtime.

As I talked to Roy outside the Kalkadoon Tribal Council Musem at Mt Isa, he spoke of his lost tribal past. He told me how his grandmother, a tribal woman, had given birth to a fair-skinned baby who became his mother.

"See, there's a long story there," he said. "My mother Elizabeth took the name 'Malarvy', and some years ago I read a book about Campbell Miles, who's known as the discoverer of Mt Isa mine —"

He broke off here to say that there were many Aborigines who were around Mt Isa at that time who emphatically disputed the claim that Campbell Miles was the discoverer. Roy pointed beyond the mine to a rocky red hill. "That's the hill, I'm told, where copper was first discovered by a stockman from Yelvertoft Station, who then showed it to Miles." He paused. "Well," he said, taking up his story again, "Miles had a bloke working for him by the name of Malarvy, and from what I can gather he was my mother's father, although I doubt that he would have claimed me as his grandson. He went away. I heard about this when I was trying to trace a bit of my history and talking to some older people. Anyway, somehow my mother and father met and I was born on the 1st January 1931 on Headingly Station, in my grandmother's country."

And what had life to offer a youngster like Roy, I thought as we sat outside the Museum, watching cars, trucks and tourist buses whizzing past on the busy highway that links the eastern half of Australia to the red centre, the Kimberley and the West.

Roy pointed over the top of another red hill strewn with boulders and spinifex. The summer heat was already making a bluish haze like a mirage around it. "I worked on a station way out there," he said.

As I took in the scene around me, gazing towards the huge structure of the mines, my eyes rested on a thick plume of dirty, reddish brown smoke that funneled up from the high smokestack, then seemed to fall back towards the earth as though it was too heavy to rise. But it drifted off towards the south-west.

Roy continued his story. "I recall that in 1937 I went to school in Camooweal for a while, then my father went to Djarra with a drover and got a job there, so we moved. A little bit more schooling for me, then about 1939 my father got a job on Carandotta Station at a water-hole called Walkaby. His job was to see drovers through. We had no quarters, no huts or anything, only our own tent. We carried water from the river. No paddock for the horses, they were hobbled out and it was the job of us kids to get the horses each morning. Sometimes Dad would be gone for a few days, travelling with the drovers, hunting away the station cattle in case they became mixed with the travelling mob — or the boss drover decided to pick up a few bullocks for meat at the station's expense.

"While Dad was away us kids would have to check his dingo trap. We could do that all right and kill and scalp the dingo, if there was one trapped, but we couldn't reset the trap — its jaws were too strong for us to open up. So we had to get Mum to do that.

"They were pretty good times, I thought. Dad would catch plenty of fish and salt them, because when the river ran there was no way you could catch anything — the fish didn't seem to bite. We had plenty of rice, too, and sometimes goanna and other bush tucker.

"At Walkaby I remember one time the police came out to our camp looking for two Aboriginal men who had talked back to some white fella in Djarra. Alec and Val, they were called. Well, when the police arrived looking for these men, Alec and Val went bush in the Channel country. The policeman told Dad, 'You find them men, tell Alec we got his wife and kids at station, gonna send 'em Palm Island. Bring him in tomorrow or he won't see them again.' Well, the police left and Dad told those men what happened, so Alec went with Dad to see the police. Dad owned a sulky, that was how we got around. I never saw Alec again until 1953 — he and his family were sent to Palm Island. Just because he argued with a white fella! Val was single — he stayed lost until he got a job with a drover passing through. He went south, stayed there for years, but he escaped Palm Island.

"Well, after a while we moved to Rockwood, an outstation on Carandotta — there was a boundary rider's hut there. And from there my Dad moved into Mt Isa, to give my younger sister some education, leaving my older brother George and me on Carandotta. George was now working in the mustering camp. The head stockman, Jubilee Page, was another well-known Aborigine. My first job was that of gate-boy for the manager. I rode around with him in his car and opened gates. At night I had a room all to myself in the blacksmith's shop, a long way from the house. It had no door. At meal times I walked up to the kitchen, where I was handed tucker on a rusty old tin plate. My chair was the woodheap, my table the ground, but it was my first job and I stayed at it for about a year.

"Then one day Dad arrived from Mt Isa. He had heard that me and George had been placed under the Act, which meant roughly — plenty work, no pay, no rights — the government owned us."

Roy was talking about the Aboriginal Act. If an Aborigine was placed under the Act, it meant that they were totally controlled by the government's local agent. They had to work where they were told, and they had no choice of the sort of work they did or where they lived. No human rights.

"Well, Dad soon sorted that out somehow," Roy told me. "He got my brother and me all the back pay coming to us and took us both to the Isa with him. That was my first cheque. As we drove into town, Dad said to me: 'A bit more schooling won't hurt you.' So I went back to school in Mt Isa.

"At the beginning of 1946 I finally left school and went straight out to work at a place called Carlton Hills Station — out there." Roy pointed across the spinifex-covered hills towards the north. "I was ringing there for a while until I went on my first droving trip with a mob of cattle from Walgra, on the Georgina River, to Werner Station. I got a job on Werner and stayed there for a time, doing everything from mustering to milking. It was a pretty good job really."

"What about wages?" I asked.

"Well, when my brother and the other young Aboriginal fellas were working in the mustering camp on Rocklands, they was all getting thirty bob a week. I was pretty well liked, see, and I was getting five pounds a week, so I was doing all right. But after a while on Werner I became restless. I wanted to travel around a bit, see the country, so I pulled out."

And wander around on horseback was what Roy did: over the next few years he worked on stations, broke in horses, and his droving trips took him from the sprawling unfenced pastures of Victoria River Downs through the dreaded Murrinji scrub across the Barkly Tableland and down into the Channel country of south-west Queensland, where Coopers Creek sometimes floods sixty miles wide, right into the busy trucking yards at Quilpie.

These yearly droving trips were controlled by the huge pastoral companies, which owned vast tracts of land across the north, where the cattle were bred a long way from the southern markets. Many of the companies had fattening properties in the Channel country, for here, after the flooding rains, were the lushest natural grazing pastures in the world. Every year, the drovers brought thousands of

young steers to graze, then after fattening they were taken
to the railheads at Quilpie, Winton, Bourke or Broken Hill,
and down the Birdsville Track to Maree in South Australia.

Roy told me about one trip he made in 1947 when he was
sixteen. "Me and my brother George, William Barton and
Danny Daley worked for a drover called Henry Morris. We
mustered his horses at Urandangi — he had about seventy
of them. It was real hot weather and we took those plant
horses to Morstone Station, owned by the Vesty mob. There
we picked up one hundred station horses we had to take to
Helen Springs. Well, we had to hobble our seventy plant
horses at night — that was okay, but we also had to watch
the hundred station horses day and night. I remember one
day on dinner camp, we was all relaxing as the horses fed
around us, when all of a sudden the station horses took off.
Flat-out they went. We blocked up most of them, but about
forty were still going, making for home. Morris and my
brother went after the galloping horses. They got them all
right, and came back to the camp about twelve o'clock that
night.

"After we delivered the horses we had twelve hundred
head of cattle to take back to Morstone. My brother was
cooking — I recall that was the first time I seen these
packhorse drovers' cooks. They cooked enough corn meat
and damper to last three days, because there was no wood,
only cow-dung fires. Coming off watch at night it was
sometimes cold and there was no bloody warmth at all from
them cow-dung fires. Well, we delivered the cattle at Morstone.

"Then I got a job for a while on Avon Downs. There were
two camps, Avon Downs and Wave Hill. From what I could

gather they hadn't mustered that country for years. It was full of big old clean-skins, thousands of them. There may have been six or seven white stockmen and about forty Aboriginal stockmen in the two camps. It was all bronco work, branding them clean-skins. One Aboriginal stockman I recall from there was a bloke called Tommy Dodd. One day I watched him saddle up a mare and get on her, and didn't she buck! But she had no chance of throwing him. I heard later there were people who would've backed Tommy Dodd to ride any horse in Australia out in the bush — he was a great horseman. I think they took about 3000 cattle back to Wave Hill after the muster. Peter Pedrill was head stockman on Avon. The tucker was all right and they were a pretty good mob of men to work with.

"I came back to the Isa, and next year I was doing nothing, so I got a ride with the Vesty's road boss — McIntosh, he was called. We were sure to meet up with some drover coming in short-handed — you could always find a job then. The road boss left me at Anthony's Lagoon. I stayed there the night, and next day I had my first ride in an aeroplane, a real little one, from there to Brunette Downs. I wasn't very sure about accepting that plane ride — a bit frightened, ya know. Well, the manager at Brunette Downs told me a drover had passed by that day, so after supper he took me down to the camp. From there I got a job droving from Brunette Downs to Morstone with Charlie McKenzie. He had his wife with him — they had a pack-horse plant and she done the cooking and helped with the cattle. (In fact, I think she wore the trousers in that camp.) We had about 1,300 cattle and it was a pretty good trip. After that I kept droving and working in mustering camps until 1949, when I went down south into the Channel country."

* * *

In 1949, Roy told me, he went on his first big droving trip working for Walter Cowan from Rocklands station, near Camooweal, to Tanbar on Coopers Creek.

"We had 1,250 head of cattle. That was a pretty good trip — it lasted about three months. From Tanbar we went back to Caddapan and took a mob of fat cattle to the trucking yards at Quilpie. That lasted about five weeks, then we came straight back to Waverney Station, not far from Tanbar, and took delivery of 1,300 mixed store cattle and headed back to Quilpie again. They were a pretty bad mob, rushing almost every night. It was a terrible trip, a real experience for me. I was only eighteen at the time.

"I still remember one young night horse on that trip. He was a good horse, but if you were riding around on him on night watch and the cattle just began to move, just jumping to their feet, not rushing off camp — it was eerie, you'd hear that horse's heart beating loud and feel its vibration with your legs. That young horse must have been a nervous wreck. If there'd been a rush he would've wanted to take off the other way — that's the truth. They had to take him off night watch. Those were probably the worst cattle I have been with. They were real bad at the finish."

Roy paused. "Ya heard of a place called Orange Tank?" he asked me. "They were cutting timber there."

I nodded. "Well," he went on, "we had a bad rush there the last night on the road. Five head of cattle were killed — they had their shoulders almost torn off in the rush. So we was really pleased to reach the trucking yard next day and get them away. That was getting close to the end of the year, so we headed back to Tanbar to move another mob of fat bullocks to Quilpie. We took delivery at Gilpeppee out-station, then headed off across the channels. But there'd been a lot of storms further upstream, and when we'd got almost across the channels the waters came flooding down. We couldn't go on, so we camped for a few days, hoping the water would drop. But it rose even higher. Walter decided we couldn't meet the trucking date, so we turned back — only to discover that all the channels behind us had flooded. Then, fearing that we could be trapped in them channels for months, we let the cattle go.

"Walter showed us how to make a boat out of three horse packs, a piece of wood and our calico tarpaulin. Me being the only one who could swim, each channel we came to I'd swim across with a piece of string held in my teeth, onto which were tied all the surcingles, girth straps and bridle reins. Then the others would load up the canvas boat and I'd pull it across. Then, as we didn't have enough straps for the others to pull the boat back for the next load, I'd swim back so that the others could pull back the boat — on and on it went, until we had all the gear and men across … after which I'd have to swim back and get the fifty or so horses across. I don't know how many channels I swam all told, but there was a bloody lot of them!

"Well, we were in those channels for ten days or more, until finally we came to the last one. There was an old bronco yard there which provided plenty of wire, so that channel was easy to cross. I only had to swim across once, pull over the boat, then the others would pull it back using the wire. Then I swam the horses over for the last time and drove them up onto the bank. We were back to where we had taken delivery of the cattle what seemed like ages before … and there, camped at the gate of the bullock paddock, were all the cattle we had let go over a week before and miles away! I called out to Walter and he caught a horse and counted them back into the paddock.

* * *

We had been going non-stop droving for over six months. Alas, sad news awaited me when I returned home — I learnt that my father had died several months before. My people had sent me three telegrams asking me to return home, because when Dad knew the end was near he kept asking for me. But I never received any telegram. It was a big disappointment for me. But there is one thing I am grateful for. When Dad kept asking for me, my mate went up and pretended to be me as he sat with him. Yes, for that I am forever grateful.

"Another thing I'd like to mention here — Walter Cowan was a good bloke to work for and a great drover, yet you never hear of him being wrote about much. On that droving trip in 1949 he was supposed to be in his thirty-first year of droving from Rocklands to Tanbar. That alone must be some sort of record."

As Roy spoke, I recalled that I had met Walter Cowan in the early 1960s, still droving from Rocklands to Tanbar. Around the drovers' campfire a debate raged about who had been droving that route the longest, Walter Cowan or another drover called Jack Carrol. They were both elderly men then, and both had been droving for over forty years on that same route. Each was trying to outdo the other. When I saw Walter Cowan he was crippled up and had to use a kerosene tin or a stump to mount his horse. But mount it he did and rode off to chase that elusive record, maybe wishing each year that Jack Carrol would retire. One of these days I must find out which of them did hold the record in the end …

Roy resumed his story. "1959 was the first time I went to Victoria River Downs for cattle. I was horse tailer for a bloke called Bill Sharp. Me and Harold Condron took the plant horses from Urandangie. But first we had to go to Wave Hill and take a mob from there to Helen Springs.

"On the way out we had some trouble with the horses, and when we reached Elliot we was short of tucker. We met the boss there, then went on. One night we lost seven horses and couldn't pick up their track. Another mob of horses had passed and walked over the track, and I was looking in the wrong place. There was just no sign of them horses, so the boss left me with a good saddle horse and pack, horse tucker and swag, and said: 'Find them.'

"Well, I didn't know that country at all. As I was trying to pick up the track I ran into a mate of mine who was horse-tailing for another drover. He had picked up the two geldings, so that was okay — at least I now had two of those seven horses. Then I followed tracks out into the Never-Never towards Beetaloo. Nobody knew I was in that country, and it was all holes. Well, next day I came across another three colts. They was with a creamy brumby stallion. I had a couple of miles' gallop, but I ended up with the colts, so that was five I had.

"The day after that, about twenty miles further on, I pulled up for dinner on the edge of a plain and I see these horses feeding about, so I let my horses feed out on the plain, and soon them other horses, led by a brumby stallion, come close and I see the two missing mares, with a broken hobble strap and the hobble chain swinging like shin tapper, and I took off after them. They couldn't gallop fast with that chain swinging, and rapping them on the shin so I finally had the seven horses back.

"Then I started off after the boss and got to Top Springs. It was my first time out there and this bloke drew me a map of all the government bores and I headed off. By then the others were on their way back with the mob, so I didn't get to see Wave Hill Station itself, which was disappointing.

"But one thing I did see and will remember for ever. This strange encounter happened after I found those horses, just past the Murrinji. I camped near this Gil-gi hole. (Gil-gi holes are natural small depressions in the ground which fill after rain. Where the water lays it is sometimes crystal clear, but they soon dry up.) During the night I heard this loud panting and puffing noise next to my swag. I looked and saw what I can only describe as a round, jet-black ball of fluff. It sounded like a dog — but it didn't look like a dog. It was real big, too big for any dog. I jumped out of my swag and started pelting it with stones … It was funny, but that black ball of fluff just seemed to fade back to the Gil-gi hole and disappear. Then I would lay down, and again the panting, puffing ball of black fluff would be back. More stone throwing — believe me those stones just seemed to be going right through that thing. I was a pretty good shot with a stone, you know, but that thing got the better of me. Well, I rolled up the swag, got the horses saddled up and moved on. One or two o'clock in the morning, it musta been. That morning I met the drovers on their way back, but I didn't tell them what made me rise so early.

"Well, we delivered those cattle at Helen Springs, then went back to a place called Dashwood on Victoria River Downs, and took delivery of 1,300 cattle and started back. I was horse-tailing, see, and when you hit the Murrinji Track it's rough, really bad. When you come through there you don't let them horses out of your sight. It's real thick scrub — from fifty yards away you could ride past the horses and not see them. Ya really gotta watch cattle and horses real close. When I went out for the horses before the first streaks of dawn I would have to check the stars, otherwise you could get bushed. Ya couldn't see the glow from a campfire or a light, the scrub was that thick. What I used to do was unhobble all the horses, block off the bells, check the stars, then ride away a bit from the horses. You could mostly hear a bullock cough or the bloke on night watch singing as he rode around the herd.

"It's a strange place, that Murrinji. The only birds I saw were mostly black cockatoos — no galahs or corellas or magpies, nothing but black cockatoos. And some little kangaroo rats. It shocked me really. As for the trees, the only ones I didn't see were gydgea and snapping gum. All the rest was there — whitewood, supple-jack, all those sort of trees and plenty of bullwaddy, which the cooks used for making damper.

"I heard plenty of tales of people becoming lost along the Murrinji. They told me how one young fella got lost in the daytime when he was driving the horses back to camp. He didn't backtrack himself, just kept riding on. He ended up on the Darwin road. The drover had no fresh night horses that evening and the young fella had no tucker or swag. Other drovers had lost mobs of cattle. It's a bad place all right.

"Well, we delivered them cattle at Walgra, near Urandangi, in Queensland. It took about three months. After we delivered I went back to Mt Isa for a well-earned rest. And I took back with me the secret of that black ball of fluff that the stones seemed to go straight through. I was afraid people would laugh if I told them what I had seen. A few years later I married and then I told my wife what I had seen, and not long afterwards she showed me an old magazine with a story by some bloke who had camped at that very spot near the Gil-gi hole. He described in every detail the thing I had seen. Later still, I heard of others who had seen it too. You know, I've camped out many a night alone in the bush before and since that episode, but the only time I had to roll my swag in the middle of the night was that time in 1959, not far from the Murrinji Track. It was strange, real strange.

"Next year I was employed by Fred Hird. He had a contract to take two mobs of cattle from Victoria River Downs to Walgra, in Queensland, and wanted me to be in charge of his second droving plant. But first we had to get enough horses together. So early in the year we went to Walgra, where his horses were running. He got a few unbroken horses which we had to break in. Eventually we had about 110 horses, enough for the two plants, and we started out for Victoria River Downs, me and four others, all Aborigines. Three of them were youngsters who didn't know much. They almost had me run off my legs on the way out, hobbling and unhobbling over a hundred horses — and I was still breaking in the brumbies on the way. The boss had gone on in the truck. Well, we finally got to a place called Elbow Hole, an out-station on Victoria River Downs.

"Here we camped for a couple of weeks while waiting for the first mob of cattle. We picked up two local Aboriginal stockmen, Frank and Fred. They were real top horsemen and a real big help. Between the three of us we shod all them horses, over a hundred head. The bloke I was running the plant for never came near us — he was away somewhere using his truck to help a station bloke peg a fence line. Soon they had the bullocks mustered. By then there were other drovers waiting to take delivery of mobs, so me and Fred sorted out the horses, taking half each, and the others agreed I should take the first mob. Them old drovers were pretty good to me, telling me where to be careful, pointing out the bad spots on the stockroute. So here I was in charge of 1,580 head of cattle from Victoria River Downs to Walgra.

"Well, coming through the Murrinji I soon found out ya had to keep belting the lead back through the scrub. We was lucky we found these two young Aborigines walking through the Murrinji — some station boss had chased them off. I don't know why, because they were two good boys and they helped me to Elliot.

"When we got to Elliot this Aboriginal Affairs bloke drove up. The two stockmen from Victoria River Downs were turning back — they didn't want to go into Queensland. So the department bloke, he asked these two young fellas we'd picked up along the Murrinji Track, would they like to go into Queensland. 'Yes,' they said, so they stayed with me to Walgra. I was sorry to see the other two blokes go. They were real smart men, only for them I wouldn't have gotten through the Murrinji, because the cattle were rushing at night.

"From Elliot ya hitting the downs and then you're out of all the trouble. It was a real easy trip from there. I delivered those cattle at Walgra, then we took horses back to the Camooweal Common and let them go. I took them two young blokes back to where Fred Hird was coming in with a second mob of cattle. He paid them off and put them on a bus home. They really enjoyed their trip into Queensland.

"The next year I went back to Victoria River Downs with Bill Sharp. I done my first trip with him. We went to a place called Mt Stanford and there was another couple of drovers waiting there, and we started mustering. That was the biggest mob of cattle I have ever seen at one time. There were some men holding cattle, others mustering, and horses — they were everywhere, hundreds of them. At night there would be eight men on watch at once. It was unreal. I remember at Mt Stanford one night the cattle rushed — there were over 3,000 head and my God, didn't they make a terrible noise! Luckily we were camped on open flat ground, with eight of us on watch to block them up.

"Well, we finally started drafting out the mob — cattle, horses and men everywhere. There were about 1,500 head for each drover, and as each mob was drafted off, the drover and head stockman would ride through the cattle with an old lever-action rifle, look at some shelly old bullock, say 'He won't make it to Queensland,' and shoot him on the spot. They shot plenty. A bullet behind the shoulder until the mob looked okay.

"You know, I can't say how many men were mustering there that year with all the drovers, but there were only a few white blokes, a handful really. All the rest were Aboriginal stockmen, all smart men too. It made me wonder, you know. I'm sure them Aboriginal stockmen could've done that job without the aid of the few whites. But there was no way them whites could've done the job without the Aboriginal stockmen.

"I asked them blokes about pay. They said they got couple shirts and trousers, pair of riding boots each year. 'What about Christmas — you go to town?' 'No way,' they told me. They were driven out to a waterhole, a few bullocks were killed, and there they stayed living off the land until they were needed the next year.

"Well, eventually we started off with our 1,500 head of cattle and they began rushing before we got to the Murrinji, so we held them back, trying to quieten them down a bit, and in the end we got them to Walgra.

"After they were delivered I took a job at Walgra, at a place called Munta Bore, about twenty miles from the station. Weather was getting hot and my job each day was to start the diesel motor to pump the water to the surface. The windmill rods were disconnected because the wind couldn't be relied upon to work the pump. There was a lot of cattle there. I lived in a small tent with a little bough shed — no fridge, no telephone, I hardly saw anyone. They would send out a bag of salted meat and there was plenty of tea and sugar, flour, potatoes and onions and tobacco. I had an old rifle and shot a few pigeons when they came to water. I spent Christmas there alone. By then it was very hot and in the evening the dust storms would blow up, and the only thing I could do was get in the tent and wrap myself in a blanket. The dust was that thick it was almost impossible to eat — all you ate was dust.

Eventually some thunderstorms started to fall further away from the bore and the cattle disappeared for a while — they went chasing the storms. Well, about a week later I saw this thick plume of red dust coming from the north. It was strange, I couldn't make out what this big red-dust cloud was. It turned out to be over a thousand bullocks trotting towards me, tongues hanging out, panting and puffing. It was terrifying! I raced over to the water trough, undid the float and let the water flow out, at the same time trying to keep the cattle away. I was afraid they would wreck the trough. They'd smelt the storms fall in the far corner of that vast paddock, walked out there, and found a bit of surface water scattered around, but when that dried up they were stuck miles from any other water. Ya know, they weren't far from perishing, them bullocks. But everything turned out okay, eventually it did rain and the Georgina flooded. Then I was stranded and never saw anyone for a couple of months. Luckily I had plenty of tucker and tobacco. I finally got to the station in February, then headed back for the Isa.

"Over the years I kept working on stations and droving in the north-west. I remember a few droving trips well. One, in 1954, was from Brunette Downs to the trucking yards at Djarra with 700 fat cattle. We had a young Aboriginal stockman called Calico working with us. I'd met him the year before — he had come into Morstone from the Ord River or some place out there in Western Australia. After we trucked them cattle at Djarra and brought the horses back to Camooweal, ya should've seen Calico when he was given his cheque! Must have been the first time he was paid his worth and treated fairly. He musta felt like a millionaire.

"Another droving trip that year, me and my mate Charlie Perue worked for this bloke taking fats from Walgra to Djarra. This boss was one of the worst bastards I worked for. I watched him one night waking a man for night watch — he didn't call him, just walked up to the swag and kicked the bloke in the guts and abused him. Well, after we trucked the cattle he bought lots of rum, and when us fellas got drunk, including me, he bashed shit out of us. He left us at the trucking yards with no pay. So I sobered up and went up to the pub, where this boss drover had just knocked out Charlie with a piece of wood because he had asked for his pay. So then me and the boss ended up fighting. I got the best of him, gave him a few kicks in the mouth and guts because he'd done the same to me when I was drunk. When the policeman arrived he didn't say much. He had a look at my mate, who was still out to it, and the boss drover groaning on the ground and he said to me: 'You look after your mate,' so I did. That policeman must of said something to that drover, for shortly after we were told our money was at the police station. Ya know, I've been very lucky in life, been working mostly for good people, but that drover was one bad fella. I recall he later ended up in a wheelchair — he deserved a bad end, that bloke.

"In 1957, my mother started drinking and was sent to a mission — Cherbourg, I think it was. Well, me and my brother George didn't know about this, we were working on different stations at the time. But when George found out he contacted me and said he needed some money as he was going to get Mum out of that mission. So we pooled our money and George took off. He was gone quite a while, but when he came back Mum was with him. She never drank again after that. She was very independent, living alone and caring for young relations. When she died in 1986 it was a great loss to us all. I don't know how old she was. I remember how she and her brother, a big old bloke called Muscley, would always talk in their own language when they were together.

"In 1963, while I was working around Djarra, I met my Missus and came to the Isa. Our first child was born in 1965. I was working all the time in mustering camps until finally I went to Ashover for a few months. That was the finishing of my ringing days. That would have been in 1974. Then I got a job with a contractor putting in water and sewage pipes at a housing developing in Mt Isa. That was my first job in town and it was pretty hard work. From there I got a job on the railway as a navvy. That job lasted nine and a half years, until I hurt my shoulder. I was a bit unlucky there, you know, because if that hadn't happened I would still be working on the railway today."

As he spoke, I looked at Roy's left hand, which was slightly withered from a stroke. He pulled out his battered old tobacco tin and deftly rolled a smoke. Then he handed me the tin so that I could examine the lid, decorated with a beautifully traced out horse and rider.

In the past many bushmen with time on their hands would trace and punch out sketches on the lids of tobacco tins, and Roy still practises this once-common art form. I have seen many of these tins in mustering and droving camps over the years, and I consider some true works of art.

As we talked, from inside the Kalkadoon Tribal Council Cultural Centre came the haunting sound of a didjeridoo, played by Delma Barton. It was a strange, almost eerie sound, and I realised I had never heard a woman play before. While Delma played, her husband Alfie, a Tribal Elder and longtime Telecom employee, now retired, explained to a group of tourists the purpose of the many different artifacts on display and the importance of Aboriginal culture.

My meeting with Roy was almost at an end. "What about the present — and the future?" I asked Roy.

"Well," he said, "education is something young people gotta have this day and age. As long as they still know they're Aboriginal, culture will take care of itself. Lifestyle is what worries me. But everything is slowly falling into place. For years we went backwards. What I'm really pleased about is Aborigines with education being able to stand up and speak out about shocking housing and health conditions. I don't know about all those other things, politics and the rest."

"Any regrets about the past, anything you'd want to change?"

"Not really," Roy replied. "I worked with a lot of top stockmen, a great many of them Aboriginal. One thing I really disliked was the way these top blokes used to get their tucker served up to them on a piece of bag. You know, a lot of them blokes would have been better stockmen and had cleaner habits and more principles than their white bosses. That was real bad. But on the whole I was lucky. I worked mostly for good people and was given a go. You meet good and bad in all walks of life."

Today, Roy lives in the house he moved into in 1971, where he and his wife, Mary, have raised their five children.

There remains one real mystery in Roy Mahar's life, which he would like resolved. It is the sight he witnessed that night he camped beside the Gil-gi hole, not far from the Murrinji Track, the huge jet-black ball of fluff which the stones he hurled at seemed to pass straight through. "Strange, that one," Roy said, "real strange. You know, I still wonder about that thing ..."

Archie Dick

Enemy plane, strange lights and the things you find in sugar bags

He was born at Lawn Hill Station on 10th May 1935, in a bark humpy.

"I was the oldest of ten children — eight boys, two girls. My tribe is Waanyi. My father's name was Left-handed Dick. He was a stockman, and he was also born at Lawn Hill."

"How did he get that name?" I asked.

"Well, he was a left-handed lad," Archie said. "Simple."

At that time tribal names were discouraged, so Archie, that Waanyi boy, became "Archie Dick". His mother's name was Daisy. Her mob belonged to the MacArthur River country, over the Northern Territory border. From the age of twelve, she worked as a housemaid at Lawn Hill homestead. After she married, and between having her children, she still climbed the big steep hill where the homestead is perched.

"It musta been all right coming home at night," I said. "Downhill all the way." I recalled a visit I once made to Lawn Hill, walking from the horse yards up that steep slope.

Neither of Archie's parents had any education.

"Did they get any pay from the station?" I asked him.

"Very little," he replied. "We had an old aunty, Maggie Friday, who looked after us while Mum worked. We used to get sugar, tea and flour from the homestead. There was plenty of tucker all around us — we'd go bush every day. Plenty of wild figs, honey from the wild bees — plenty of cabbage palm. We cut it up and ate the inside. Us kids used to cut the little palms for ourselves. There was plenty of fish, too; we'd cook the palm hearts with the fish in a ground oven. We ate snake, goanna and sometimes wallaby. Them old fellas used to hunt the wallaby beside the creek. One mob of hunters would go to one end and chase the wallaby towards the other mob, and then they'd let fly with their spears and boomerangs. They never missed. Them old fellas taught me to make boomerangs and spears. My father even made the tribal boomerangs — killer boomerangs they used for fighting, but I never learned how to make those properly. He would make the tribal mark on them, and they was made in the shape of the number 7. He told me that sometimes his father would pack his horse with those tribal boomerangs and head off to Lake Nash to present them to two chiefs who lived there, family relations. Archie would plead to go with him, but he never went.

"Sometimes, Mum would boil up medicine plants and us kids would bathe in a big tub and she'd add the milky medicine to the water. It stopped us getting 'flu and other things. It kept us healthy.

"They was two mobs at Lawn Hill, one on the eastern side — the workers at the station — and the others on Pages Creek camp. They was the ones that got the government handout. Sometimes these two mobs used to fight, but mostly I remember them as real happy people who enjoyed good times. The Pages Creek mob, they were the ones sent to the missions in 1938, some to Palm Island, some to Doomadgee. But some of them bolted across the Northern Territory border. Those two mobs at Lawn Hill spoke almost the same lingo, only one mob talked a little bit draggy; the Waanyi talk was slow and the others' Garawa talk was fast. The Waanyi territory was from Alexandra, Borroloola, MacArthur River."

Archie told me that sometimes all the Aborigines at Lawn Hill would make the trip across the Northern Territory border to Alexandra Station for a big meeting of the clans from Lake Nash, Borroloola and Elliot. They would walk there, hunting as they went. "Dad had a gun the boss bought him — others hunted with spears and boomerangs," he recalled.

Once, when I was up that way myself, I saw an abandoned uranium mine. It is an area rich in mineral deposits — copper, lead and zinc. The richest lead zinc mine in the world is close by the waters of the Gulf, teeming with barramundi and prawns, the fishing ground of the Gulf country. The Gregory River flows nonstop through this dry, desolate, hard-looking country, nearby scenic Lawn Hill Gorge is now a leading tourist destination. Not far to the south is Riversleigh, with its myriad fossil deposits.

"I remember them tribal dances at Alexandra," Archie said wistfully. "They'd start off with us piccaninnies a part of it, then us little fellas gone to sleep. But just before dawn they'd wake us outta sleep — 'Come on up! Everybody gotta dance!' All the men and boys from the different mobs joined in that last dance. Ooh, you oughta have heard the rattle — five or six singers, boomerangs, didgeridoos, clapsticks … Gee, I miss all that. They was real happy people then. When the corroboree was over everybody scattered — might be next time they meet at Lake Nash, Borroloola or Lawn Hill."

On one trip back home, Archie recalled that a whitefella cattle owner told one of the old tribesmen, Bumblefoot

Jack: "You want 'em meat, there's a big spade cow here on my land that belongs to another station — you fellas can kill that one. If a spade cow eats your grass, you eat that spade cow — that's the rule!" (Spade cows don't, of course, have calves, but they eat just as much grass as those that do.) "Now mind you shoot the right cow, not one of mine," he told them.

"Okay," says Bumblefoot Jack. So the boss hands him a rifle and says, "You get up that tree and we'll drive the cattle up, then you shoot."

But Barefoot Jack pushed the gun aside. "No more bumba, me shoot 'em meself in foot," he said — and Archie recalled how he took his spear and went behind a pandanus palm. As the cattle walked past, he speared that big spade cow behind the shoulder-blade.

"Swish!" said Archie, "straight through the heart. Gawd!" I could see he was still awed by that feat. "The cow was dead before she hit the ground. Oh Murrie, he was good, that old man, that Bumblefoot Jack. He used to spear crocodile to eat, too."

Archie described how he would wait at the horse paddock gate for the horse-drawn mail service from Bourketown to Alexandra. He'd open the gate and get a packet of lollies from the mailman, Paddy Rook. "But then motor transport came in and that stopped Paddy's mail service. I went with him on his last trip in the wagonette."

Archie's childhood days at Lawn Hill were carefree and happy, he told me in his slow drawl. Grey-haired now, he is short and thickset, with clear, dark eyes. When he laughs, the sound comes from deep within.

But those happy times ended in 1943, when the five eldest Dick children were gathered up and taken to the recently opened Doomadgee Mission, on the Nicholson

River. "The mission people come around in an old truck to pick us up," he said. "We had our first-ever car ride."

"What was it like at the mission?" I asked.

"Oh, not good. We didn't like the school. I didn't know what they was talking about — learning and religion and that. I hafta put the uniform on and say prayers. They was very strict. The boys used to get hit with a rubber hose and the girls got the strap. There were more girls than boys. At night, boys and girls were locked up in separate dormitories. Saturday and Sunday they let us out, girls on one side of the river, boys on the other. We went hunting. But not with the old fellas from the tribes, only with the missionaries." He paused. "I never went back to Lawn Hill for years. I never saw those old fellas who taught me to hunt. The mission teachers never allowed us to go with the old people in case they taught us the old ways, you know. Sometimes Mum and Dad came to see us, but we had to stay there. The tucker wasn't bad, but the only real thing I remember is that there were plenty of mates to play with."

Archie was fortunate that he did get to see his parents again, and was then able to work in his own country, where he kept in touch with his tribal ties, even though later on he avoided full initiation into tribal life. He preferred to adapt to present-day reality.

Archie's time at Doomadgee was during World War II, and he recalled the day the mission had a visit from a Japanese fighter plane. "All us kids in the playground saw this funny looking little aeroplane. It landed and we all raced together. We was frightened. Then it took off again and flew around. Next thing, the pilot drops a note, saying that seeing we was all little Aboriginal kids, he wouldn't harm us. There were three little white kids amongst us, and when that plane comes round again, the missionary's wife cried out: 'He's back again! I'm terrified!' Those white kids belonged to her. So then she told us all to line up and salute the aeroplane in the sky."

I imagined Archie, a chubby, round-faced kid, barefoot in red dust, his large dark eyes resisting terror as he stands to attention and salutes that Japanese plane.

"So we saluted and he waggled his wings and flew back to New Guinea. We heard later he visited Mornington Island that same day. The old boss fella, he comes out of his office, sees the plane and says, 'Oh gee, Japs!' Then he races inside and phones the Flying Fortress base — and soon five American planes come in to land."

I might add here that the only Japanese fighter pilot captured on Australian soil during World War II was in fact taken prisoner by an unarmed Aborigine. This happened about the same time as Archie's encounter with the Japanese plane. In one version, the Japanese pilot left the place where his plane came down and began wandering through the bush. The old Aborigine spotted him coming along a track and hid behind a tree. The pilot walked past the tree, and then the old man stepped out behind him and poked a short stick into his back. "Stick 'em up!" he said — just as he'd heard American cowboys give the command so many times in Western movies. The Japanese pilot raised his arms and was walked up to the nearest white man and into captivity.

"What about all those boys and girls being together there at Doomadgee?" I asked. "Wouldn't the girls be looking at the boys and the boys be looking at the girls as you got older?"

"Oh yes," laughed Archie. "That was when they kicked you out. I was there six years. I was locked up every night and I didn't learn much. I only got to Grade One." He laughed again. "I was still myall when I left."

"What happened to you then?"

"They gave me clothes, rations, and a job on Talawanta Station. I was the cowboy there."

"Not like them American cowboys galloping around and shooting off their guns?" I said.

"No, no, I just walked along on an old bay horse — his name was Memory. I learned to ride on that quiet old horse. Phil Salmon was the boss there and he give me a few lessons — how to saddle up. He told me not to gallop. Every evening I used to bring in them eight cows I looked after. I'd milk them in the mornings, and use the old separator to make butter and cream. I finished up real good at doing that," he said with pride. "Then sometimes I'd help the gardener, or go for the meat, or mess about the house. That's an Australian cowboy's job. I enjoyed it."

"After the first year at Talawanta they made me a stock-man, and I had my first buster off a horse the first day I left the cows. The boss put me on a fresh horse called Magic. He was bucking away and the boss was yelling 'Hang onto the monkey strap, hang onto the monkey strap!' The next minute I'm on the ground." Archie gave his deep laugh once more. "I stayed there three years. They was all Murries working there. The boss didn't like to have white people, his own colour, working for him. If he was asked 'You want whitefellas?' he'd say 'No, no, only Aborigines' — he reck-oned they were better workers, better stockmen than white-fellas.

"While I was there I never went near Doomadgee or Lawn Hill. I felt happy. I went to Normanton a couple of times for the races. Our money was all paid into the bank, and we'd go to the police station to get it out. One by one, in we'd go. The policeman asks, 'Where you work? How old are you?' You tell him, then policeman say, 'You under the Act,' and he'd tell you: 'No drinking, don't go near the pub — if you do you're a goner.' I only went to the shop for lollies and ice-cream," Archie said with a chuckle.

"From Talawanta I went to work on Boomarra as a stockman. It was there I had my first drink of rum. The first year, when we was camped at the homestead, I used to watch these three old Aboriginal stockmen going straight up to the big house after dinner, and I used to think, gee, where those old chaps going? Well, the second year I was there I was invited up with them old fellas and given my first nip of rum by the boss, then told to get out. Those old fellas, though, they used to sit there with their feet up, talking away over maybe two bottles of rum. They was the boss's best working men, good old fellas to work with.

"They told me that one time when they were drinking with the boss, the old white cook came into the room holding a big enamel mug, wanting rum. But the boss tell him, 'Get out, Colin, no rum for you.' Then the cook called him a 'blackfella bastard', something like that, whereupon the boss looked around for something to hit him with — anything except the rum bottle. There was a big slab of corn meat on a tray — he grabbed that, threw it, and it dropped the cook cold. Then the boss retrieved the corn meat and filled the Murries' glasses."

Archie grinned as he recounted this story, and went on to tell me how some time later, the boss walked into the kitchen and saw the cook with a pipe in his mouth and saliva dripping into the dish of dough he was mixing. The boss promptly picked up the dish and upended the mixture over the cook's head. Two hilarious episodes which took place during his time on Boomarra, with great stockmen as his tutors.

He was still at Boomarra when his father died and his mother went to live at Doomadgee. So Archie went back to Lawn Hill for the first time since he'd been taken away as a kid.

"I was happy at first," he told me. "On Sundays we used to walk around the old camp and it brought back good memories. Then I went to Doomadgee to see Mum, and she told me I gotta go through a ceremony up Borroloola way with this old uncle of mine. But I took off before he could get the chance to put the hair belt on me. I knew I was a goner once they did that — you could never run away from them then, you belonged to the tribe and its law. So I blasted off. I had to keep my eyes open in case they got me. I headed off for Bourketown."

"Then I got a job on Barkly Downs, in a big mustering camp. There were about thirty of us, mostly Murries, only a few whites. It was all bronco horses — branding time. That was a good place to work, we cut our own tucker there. At other places I been they tell us it was whitefella law — blackfella can't handle tucker, even though we was cleaner than some whites. We was under the Act, see.

"I stayed at Barkly three years, and at the end of the first season I asked the boss if I could stay on. I helped to pump water, living alone in a little hut. Next year he asked, 'You wanta go home for Christmas?' — 'No, I want pumping job.' Then the boss asked me why I didn't want to go home. — 'Nothing, boss,' I told him, 'I just want to stay on here.' I didn't tell him the reason I had to stay away from home. I knew that once you got to a certain age, you weren't allowed to go through that initiation ceremony. They never came for me, and my time was up, I became too old for what they did.

"From Barkly Downs I went out with a drover called Nat MacNamara, taking cattle from Lake Nash back to the station. One night, near the boundary rider's hut, Nat said: 'Well, Arch, he might appear tonight; I'll wake you if I see anything.' He was always telling me about the strange light he seen lotta times when he was camped around that place at night. A bit later, I heard him trotting into camp on the night horse. 'Arch, Arch!' he calls out, 'he's coming!' So then we sit at the fire watching this strange light, like a single car headlamp, coming towards a grid, heading towards us following the road. As he comes closer the light gets smaller and smaller, until it finishes up just a little red light like that" — and here Archie pointed to the tip of his little finger. He shook his head. "Gee, it was strange — it turned towards Barkly Downs once it reached the grid and went away. And when it did — gee whiz, it just seemed to open up into a brilliant beam of light. You could see number eighteen bore, the windmill and blades, all illuminated in the dark from seven miles away. Old Nat, he watched it without saying a word. As for the cattle, they never moved or took any notice of it. Then Nat says, 'What is it?'— 'I haven't a clue,' I replied.

"Once I felt safe to return home, I worked on Bothorn Station in my own area for a few months, then went pack-horse mustering for Fred Hird at Cliffdale. That was ti-tree forest country, running onto the coastal tidal flats, with plenty of big freshwater lagoons covered with lilies. Antbed ground, no fences, lotta cleanskin cattle. Oh, they was lively like hawks — we had to throw nearly every one of them, making up a mob as we went. Then we put 'em in the yard and trucked them straight away, and come back to start again. In between we done two droving trips between Lawn Hill and Roxborough Downs.

"It was while I was working with Fred that I got married, after a lotta wrangling with my relations — 'wrong meat,' they told me. Later on me and my wife split up. After that I went droving with Stan Fowler for two years, taking cattle from Avon Downs in the Northern Territory to South Galway, on Coopers Creek. We walked them cattle into Camooweal, then trucked them to Mt Isa, where we put them on a train to Julia Creek. Then we walked them past Kynuna, Winton, Stonehenge, Jundah, Windorah — about a three-month trip. During all that time the cattle only rushed once, near Jundah. A rattly old truck came past and started 'em galloping.

"Each time we done that trip, after we got to South Galway we'd take a mob of fat bullocks into Quilpie trucking yards — that took another month. That was the first time I got proper money, a full pay cheque in my hand. The boss paid me full wages, same as everyone else. No more government hand-out. It was good, droving in them days.

"In between droving trips I worked at contract mustering for a cattle buyer around Cresswell, Malapunya, Seven Emus. It was all Murries running that plant. Then I got a job for a contractor putting in grids and guideposts on the highways. That lasted eighteen months. His name was J.A. Bethel, better known as 'Blackfella Bethel'."

"What they call him that for?" I asked.

"Well, he only have us Murries working for him mostly."

"What was he like to work for?"

"Oh, he was a real old way-back ringer, a good boss — good pay for Northern Territory, too, real proper wages. He had a white foreman but he didn't like living in the bush. So I was made foreman — don't know how I got to that!" Archie laughed. "There was one old white man in our camp, he was the handyman. Well, we done all the work, from Tennant Creek east to the Queensland border and south to Alice Springs shire boundary, then north to the Newcastle Waters boundary. Gee, that was the hardest I ever worked — all crowbar and shovel jobs, no machinery, not even for mixing cement. We used a tin sheet on the ground and mixed it with shovels. We also put in three big stock tanks along the Barkley stockroute. Oh gee, don't talk about nuts and bolts! I was sick of 'em after doing them big iron tanks."

Archie recalled a strange little incident that took place at that time. "The boss sometimes brought out his kids to our camp. Well, one night we were all resting when one of these kids gets up and walks in his sleep. He goes over to a little bush and starts patting it and talking to it in a cooing voice. As we watched he walked back, then he woke up. 'What ya doing?' we asked. — 'Oh, I been patting that pet cow laying there' — and he pointed to the dark shape of the bush.

"One day I was drinking with a Murrie whose people owned a gold mine. He told me his mother was sick in Melbourne, and then he said: 'Come for a drive. Come to Melbourne. I gotta see her.' So we went to North Mulga, where there was a big Murrie camp with humpies and tents. (South Mulga was where the mission house mob lived.) He said to me: 'You got your swag? — No, leave it, you won't need it, sell it to one of these Murries.' But none of them got any money, so I gave it to my closest relation there.

"Next morning we went over the Queensland border and come through Boulia, Winton, Jundah, Quilpie, Cunnamulla — we picked up an opal gouger there — Bourke, Dubbo, Shepparton — and finally we got to Melbourne. We only pulled up along the way for a feed or a sleep, and we was drinking as we went.

"It was my first time in the city. After a while I finished up broke, so I got a job with the Burnie Board factory in Melbourne. I started by sweeping the floor. Soon as I had a job I got a room at Gordon House, down Little Bourke Street. I didn't like Melbourne — it was too cold. Didn't like the job either, but it was the only one I could find. I couldn't get over it when I first saw the city. I had to catch a tram to work — I could never get a seat and always stood hanging onto a strap.

"I stayed there nine months, just going from Gordon House to the factory and back again, and to the Olympic Hotel to drink. That was all the distance I travelled."

"Why?" I asked.

"I was too frightened I might get lost. I used to go to the pub with an old whitefella I met. We'd have a few beers and listen to the Hawking Brothers singing there. I'll never forget the first time I wanted to cross a street. There was a lotta traffic and I was waiting for it to stop. Oh shit! It just never eased."

"Weren't there traffic lights and other people crossing over?" I asked.

"Well," Archie said, "I was just standing there, watching this policeman and wondering what the bastard was doing there in the middle of the road, dancing and waving his arms about."

We both laughed as Archie, wearing riding boots and his Akubra hat, gave an imitation of that active policeman directing the city traffic. I remembered the first time I saw a traffic policeman in action, years ago — I too stood there watching, fascinated by his antics.

"It was too much for me," Archie went on, "all them people and traffic. I thought I'd never get across that street. Better to go back to Gordon House and have a camp. But bugger it — I made up me mind, I *had* to get across, so I dived into the big mob and reached the other side.

"Another thing, in the city I was always looking for someone to ask where the sun rose — you could only see a little bit of it there." He pointed to about ten o'clock in the sky. "I thought, if I ask these whitefellas they might think 'this fella's a bit queer'. Anyway, one day I was going to the pub when I saw a Murrie coming along and we started talking on the street. I asks him, 'Hey, you belong here?' — 'No, bud-a, I come from Thursday Island.' — 'Oh shit, I'm from the Gulf of Carpentaria, Bourketown way.' So anyway, I had to bung it on him for which way the sun rose in the city." Archie laughed as he recalled the other fellow's astonished look reaction. 'Oh Bud-a, I don't know which way the sun rises. I never seen it rise here.' Oh God, I'll never forget that, the way his eyes bulged as he shook his head and said: 'Bugger this, I been here months and I don't know, Bud-a.' "

"Eventually I saved some money and decided to head home, but I only got as far as Swan Hill and then I got on the grog. I found a job patching up the road. It lasted about three years. That's when I met Ron Casey, the boxer — he had the pub at Deniliquin, and all day long he shouted me free grog."

"What! How come?" I asked.

"Well, me and a mate found this baby in a bag on the river bank. We was drinking on the New South Wales side of the river when he says, 'Gee, there's something over there — look, probably a cat in the bag. Let's get it — it's a good bag.' So I grabbed a stick and was gonna whack the cat as my mate emptied it out. But he shouted: 'Gee, it's a piccaninny!' It was a live baby girl, about ten months old. We took her to the Victorian police, and we thought that would be the end of it. But we had to go to court three times, in Wentworth and then Deniliquin, and that's how I met Ron Casey. You see, that baby had been stolen. I knew her mother. The whitefella that stole the child got seven years in gaol. That was in about 1972."

"I wonder where that little girl is today," I said. "She'd be in her twenties now."

"Don't know," Archie said. "But I often wonder about her.

Well, then I decided to head home once more, so I bought a train ticket to Brisbane and set off. I had to change trains at Sydney, and I was waiting on the platform for the Brisbane train when this railway man came up. 'Where you going, mate? Brisbane? Oh gee, you're on the wrong platform, you have to cross over, you better hurry, only got a few minutes!' Well, I made it to Brisbane and had a few days there, then went on to Townsville, and took another train to Hughenden. I got a job there on the railway line for a few months, then went on to Doomadgee, and after that I got a job at Diamantina Lakes."

At this point I myself entered into Archie's story. After working at Diamantina Lakes, he and another mate of ours,

Mick, decided to go to Windorah. They was both chequed-up, and they bought a car, paying cash for it. But Archie can't drive, and Mick was too drunk to drive. I had just finished working on a station, so I said, "I'll drive you fellas home, I'm going to Cunnamulla." I was half-pissed too. Well, we stocked up on petrol and grog — not much tucker — and started off. Near Stonehenge I tried to teach Archie how to drive, but we nearly crashed into another car, so that was the end of the lesson. We went on past Jundah — there'd been some rain, so we took the bottom road and camped that night. But the rain set in and we were bogged in that black soil. We sat down until the grog ran out, then walked barefoot to an out-station six miles away, then went another few miles to a bitumen road.

I reminded Archie of that trip to Windorah, and he smiled. "Yes, that was the end of the trail for me. I been in south-west Queensland ever since and I'll be here a long time yet. Best place in the world out here."

"I got a job on Caddapan after that," Archie told me, "I stayed there for three years, then I spent six years at Galway Downs. In between I done a few short droving trips with Johnny Stewart from Davenport Downs Morney and from Tanbar to the trucking yards at Windorah. One time between jobs I ended up at Boulia and camped down the creek. Johnny Stewart was in town looking for a drover, and they told him I was there, so he heads straight down and I went with him. We took cattle to Nappa Merrie Station."

"Is that the time you was a film star?" I asked.

"Yer, yer, that's the time."

That droving trip was filmed by the ABC for the TV documentary programme "A Big Country". I recall watch-

ing the programme and thinking, "I know some of these
blokes", and the next minute, sitting in the flickering light
of the campfire, I saw my old mate Archie. But for that
firelight his dark face would have melted into the darkness
of the night.

In his slow drawl, Archie told me about an unusual
incident one night during that trip. On all cattle camps the
horse-trailer takes the first watch at night, then comes back
to roll out his swag.

"One night," Archie said. "I went to wake the boss.
'What's wrong, Arch?' he asks. — 'Hey, come and have a
look at this. Gee, I wish I had a camera!' I said. For here's
this baldy-faced bullock doubled up beside this old Murrie
at the foot of his swag. That bullock camped with the same
old Murrie a few times after that. He'd wait until the
horse-trailer finished his watch and rolled out his swag,
then he'd walk over from the herd and camp beside the old
fella.

"That trip took about three months. It was the last time
I went droving."

Archie has spent the last twenty-two years in south-west
Queensland. Today he works driving the tractor that pulls
the cook's cart from camp to camp at Nargilco Station. He
is content, aware now of aches and pains, the legacy of
untold busters and kicks. Too slow these days to mount a
bucking colt, he prefers to ride the tractor and prepare
meals for a dozen or so stockmen, black and white.

"It's a far cry from the days when they told you that under
the act blackfellas mustn't touch the tucker!" he said.
"There's been a lotta changes over the years, Herb — things
aren't like they were before. Pay, good jobs, the way we're
treated, education, health — it's all changing for the better.
I reckon it's all right for Murries to live in a nice house today.

They could never get good jobs or done that in times gone by." He paused, then said: "We must have reconciliation — there's only one Australia and we all gotta get along. But I reckon we should think about it a bit more. There may be something wrong about what's going on right now."

I asked Archie if he could name one outstanding stockman and horseman he had come across, but he said he'd seen too many, both Aboriginal and non-Aboriginal, to single out just one. But he did say that most of the best of them were the Aboriginal stockmen.

So I came to the end of my conversation with this short, thickset man from the Waanyi tribe. Long ago he had watched a tribal elder kill a big spade cow with one thrust of his spear — and he had stood to attention, barefoot in the dust, to salute a Japanese plane. He had seen the mysterious Min-Min light; he had hesitated at the kerbside in a city street, afraid to go across. He had rescued a baby by the riverside. And today he is still employed in the place he loves best — the Australian bush.

Archie Dick had told me so much ... but he left much more unsaid.

Beyond that high hill where Lawn Hill homestead stands are the graves of two men. One has a monument, the other is unmarked. One is the grave of a white policeman; the other is the resting place of an Aborigine who is said to have been tipped into it upside-down. How these two men came to be buried there is part of the recorded white history of Australia. But written white history sometimes conflicts with Aboriginal oral history. The story I am about to relate is one

I have heard over many years — and I listened as Archie
Dick told it to me once again.

The events concerning those two men, the Aborigine Joe
Flick and the white senior police constable, Wavell, took
place in October, 1889. There is no doubt that at times
there were many confrontations between black and white;
the different versions about what happened will always be
open to dispute.

I have seen those two graves, and I have read the white
versions of what happened that day. I have also listened to
a number of Aboriginal versions about the events. Shortly
before I talked to Archie, my interest in the affair had been
rekindled by yet another article about it, in the *Sunday Mail*,
Brisbane, written from the white viewpoint. I now feel
compelled to set down this Aboriginal version of those
events.

Back in 1899, a white person could shoot twenty or thirty
Aborigines and expect to go free. Yet if one white was killed,
many Aborigines, men, women and children, might be
murdered in retaliation. British justice did not apply to
Aborigines in the law courts, even though the blacks were
often more truthful and possessed greater dignity than
many of the whites who gave evidence there. Too often
justice was dispensed through the barrel of a gun, by
so-called superior beings. In retrospect, far from any superior intelligence, it seems that it was the gun itself that
imposed its will upon Aboriginal Australians.

This, then, is the Aboriginal version of the drama played
out that October day.

Young Joe Flick walked into the bar of a grog shanty near
Turnoff Lagoon, kept by a man and wife by the name of
Cashman. When Joe asked for a drink, he was abused by
Mrs Cashman, who told him in no uncertain terms: "We

don't serve blacks here." Now Flick was a crack shot with a revolver. He was also heartily tired of the uppity attitudes of the whites and the treatment they handed out to Aborigines. He pulled out a pistol and fired a single shot. It was said to have parted the woman's hair without touching her head. She fainted on the floor, whereupon Flick walked around to the bar, stepped over her prone body and helped himself to a few bottles of hard liquor. Then he walked out, mounted his horse and rode to Lawn Hill Station. There he had a dispute with the manager, whose name was Hann, and holed up in the storehouse.

When the manager came to the storehouse door and asked to talk to him, he promised Flick that he would come in unarmed. So Flick opened the door and let him in, but immediately Hann tried to draw his gun — he had concealed it in the top of his boot — and shoot him. Flick, however, was too fast on the draw for Hann; he shot him through the chest, wounding him. Then he slammed the storehouse door shut, leaving the manager outside. The wounded Hann was helped to cover by a native policeman called Bob Killer.

Senior police constable Wavell and a blacktracker called Noble — it was said he could shoot the eye out of a needle — were both taking part in the siege. It was at this point that Wavell was shot and died instantly.

The siege continued. By this time Flick was getting short of bullets. He asked the houseboy, Nym, to get him a fresh supply from the homestead, but Nym refused — so Flick shot him dead. After that, one of the homestead housemaids — her name was Jenny — got the ammunition Flick wanted and the siege continued. Flick was wounded in the leg. During the night, he managed to escape down the rugged cliff face to the creek, and sought refuge in a thick patch of cane-grass that grew there.

When it was discovered that Flick had escaped from the storehouse, the black trackers soon saw that he had been wounded, and they trailed him to that patch of cane-grass. But here was another stand-off: at first, no one, black or white, would go in there to flush out Flick. Then Tracker Noble agreed to go in alone. He broke off a stick about two feet long and placed his hat on it. Holding the stick away from his body and above him, he entered the high cane-grass, stalking Flick. He crawled and crouched as he went, sometimes stopping to wait, always alert. In all probability, Tracker Noble would have told himself that only he or Joe Flick would emerge from that cane-grass alive. Both were crack shots.

The remainder of the police and the black trackers waited silently.

They did not have to wait long. Two shots in quick succession came from the cane-grass. After the first shot, the onlookers saw Noble's hat punched into the air, tossed above the cane-grass by the force of the bullet from Flick's gun. The second shot came almost simultaneously from Noble's gun. He then retreated and told the watchers that he had not actually seen Flick.

After Flick had fired, Noble could see nothing — no movement, only a blue wisp of smoke rising amid the dense growth. He took aim and fired below that rising smoke. He felt sure that he had hit Flick. Then he retired to safety.

No one would enter that cane-grass to verify that Flick was in fact dead. As the hunters pondered their next move, one of them had a brainwave: why not bring him out using the age-old Aboriginal method of hunting prey in long grass — set fire to it and wait for Flick to emerge? So, with a fresh south wind blowing, the cane-grass was set alight, and flames soon raced through the tinder-dry growth. But no Joe Flick emerged out of the smoke and flames. The hunters were left staring at the blackened piece of land and smouldering stubble, where nothing moved except a few half-cooked lizards and snakes.

Finally they went looking for Flick, and soon found his body, with his clothes smouldering. He was dead after all.

But it was not that fire, nor was it the leg wound he suffered that ended the short life of Joe Flick, the supposedly murderous outlaw. Perhaps he was a true freedom fighter for justice and equality, tired of the attitudes of whites and the rule of their guns. Killed by one of his own race.

In my own travels I have met a lot of prejudiced people, the same sort who long ago created the climate for the likes of Joe Flick to seek their own brand of justice, for when, ignorance is combined with arrogance, it brings out the worst in any race, black or white. And, as I say elsewhere in this book, when the real history of this great land is told, and when the great Aboriginal leaders stand tall and the white historians accept the truth about the black past, only then can we hope to come to terms with present disputes and plan a better future for all, regardless of race, colour or religious belief. Many races try to create false images of themselves through propaganda. Fanatics and murderers, geniuses and criminals are born of every race — and fair-minded people accept this fact.

Who were the real heroes and villains of this drama? Was Joe Flick looking for a runaway woman, as some have suggested — and was she the housemaid, Jenny, who supplied him with fresh bullets? Perceptions of heroism and villainy are mingled in this tale and confused by the dual

versions of white and black. Joe Flick has been called a
"black outlaw" by white historians, but I prefer to think of
him as a freedom fighter. What comparison is there between Joe Flick and a white outlaw such as Ned Kelly, who
was a murderer and criminal? Was Nym, the houseboy, a
hero or villain when he refused to get bullets for Flick? Was
Noble a heroic tracker or the murderer of a freedom
fighter? And what about the native policeman Bob Killer,
who rescued the wounded Hann after he had tried to
deceive Flick?

Afterwards, in the place where the cane-grass had stood,
the ground was ploughed for vegetable gardens. Symboli-
cally, one garden belonged to a relative of Archie Dick's —
the other was worked by a white man. Both gardens flourished, supplying produce for the station and the surrounding district, until produce was brought in by motor
transport.

Lawn Hill Station is now "foreign owned" — as some
Aborigines would have said in the days of Joe Flick. When
I visited Lawn Hill and walked around that now untended
garden plot, I was intensely aware of the memories of the
past. The Aborigines are gone from this area now, but those
memories still linger. These events were part of Australia's
history.

Both Archie Dick and I believe that only with Aboriginal
input will the true history of this continent be recorded —
not only the last 200 years, but thousands of years before
that. And only then can we hope for understanding and
peaceful co-existence.

The past can never be changed, but the future can be
shaped by people of vision and faith. When the best people
of all races combine to fight injustice and do away with

ignorance and arrogance, only then will there be true democracy and justice.

It is interesting, by the way, that Archie Dick heard about the siege of Lawn Hill from that same Corporal Bob Killer. His Aboriginal name was Bara-gud in the Northern Territory, Gul-bul-ge in Queensland, and when he was recruited into the Queensland Native Police Force from the MacArthur River area, he was given his whitefella name of Bob Killer. He eventually went to Gregory, not far from Lawn Hill, where no doubt he spent his retirement and his pension under the shadiest tree he could find. Bob Killer was in fact related to Archie's grandfather, and in the 1940s he would talk to Archie about the siege. Archie told me that when the old man knew the time of his death was near, he sent for his people to take him back to his homeland, and so Borroloola, in the Northern Territory, became his last resting place.

For me, there is always a problem: I can pronounce Aboriginal names, but spelling them is not so easy. Evidently Gul-bul-ge had the same problem, for one day a youngster who had learned to read and write at the mission came to visit the old man, and offered to write his name on his hat.

"How you say your name?" he asked.

"Gul-bul-ge."

"How you spell that, old man?"

The old Aborigine kept repeating "Gul-bul-ge", but the kid kept shaking his head. "Don't know how to spell 'em," he said, so instead he carefully wrote GOOD-BELLY on the brim of the old man's hat.

While Senior Constable Wavell's spirit must rest peaceful, weighed down by a stone monument, what of the restless spirit of Joe Flick, supposedly dumped into the earth upside down? Perhaps when both sides of the story are known, his spirit will rest in peace.

Ruby de Satge

"I been to Sydney too"

Ruby de Satge was born near Urandangi on the Georgina River. She don't know when — or refused to tell me how old she was — but I soon realised that a life of hard work had not stifled her laughter and goodwill. As we talked, a stream of relatives young and old came visiting, and many times our conversation was sidetracked, which only added to my information rather than distracting from Ruby's story.

I could calculate a guess at Ruby's age for this was not the first time I had met her. Thirty years before, at the northern end of Carandotta, at Warwick outstation, a land of stunted and sometimes poisonous gydgea trees and miles of open pebbly ridges, I had been employed as a stockman, and Ruby was taken on as cook for the all-male mustering camp. I recall my first impression: I saw the cook, wearing stockman's gear with an Akubra hat, labouring over the open fire. Then that cook took off the hat and I saw the red-and-white spotted bandana that held back her long dark hair. "A bloody woman cook!" I thought, as I gazed out at the desolate landscape.

There wasn't a tree nor even a depression in the ground for miles around. About a hundred yards from our camp, behind the boundary rider's little house, was a single square construction of unpainted corrugated iron: this was the toilet for the lot of us. Beyond the house were large cattle yards and a windmill pumping water to a huge stock tank — a new one, I assumed, still shiny. We had no truck in camp and no tent or tarpaulin rigged up, though the weather was still cool. Then I saw that the previous water tank had been cut in two — the halves, turned over, were being used to store rations and protect our swags from the dust that was starting to blow in more and more each day. Though it wasn't dust, it was sand that blew, as we soon found out. Each day we watched a red plume of dust appear out of the desert country beyond the Georgina. It blew for days.

So that was my first meeting with Ruby de Satge — and therein lies a tale in itself, for it was this very station, Carandotta, that was taken over by one Oscar de Satge, an immigrant of aristocratic background, who was given grazing rights to what became a vast pastoral holding. Oscar had two brothers, one known as the Duke, who had a beautiful Aboriginal mistress, called the Duchess. The story is told of how one day another famous pastoral and mining family, whilst discussing a suitable name in which to register their newly discovered copper mines, spied the Duchess riding up. "Oh, the Duchess," one said, and so the mine was named. Whether the nearby township of Duchess was named after this woman as well, I don't know, though it is doubtful if the white de Satges, like many other pastoral families of past days, would acknowledge or accept their Aboriginal family ties. Yet from that beginning the de Satges still survive and grow across this land, while the other de Satges returned to their ancestral lands overseas, having made a fortune in Australia.

Well, within a few weeks of my first meeting with Ruby, we moved to another outstation, and it was here I first encountered the real fury of a sand-storm. I recall one morning we were out mustering when the dust came over high in the sky, almost turning day into night. Yet it was eerie — on the ground there wasn't much wind or dust. We turned around and rode back to the homestead, and we'd barely let the horses go when the sand came blowing in. By then most of our fellas had made tracks for the nearest town. The gloomy sky never lifted and the sand was blowing like nothing I have experienced before or since. Me and another two stockmen (luckily we had a couple bottles of rum) locked the doors, and there we stayed for three days. When it was over we had no trouble shifting the dust, but the sand was piled up in the rooms, and we had to shovel it up and cart it out in buckets.

These are a few of the memories Ruby and I shared as we recalled the past. As we spoke, the news media were complaining about "the worst drought in living memory". For some it may well have been, but in the minds of others this statement seemed much exaggerated. During my research into Ruby's background, we both realised that during a time of drought almost a hundred years ago, on Carandotta alone 90,000 sheep and 10,000 cattle starved to death. It would be interesting to compare that time with the so-called "worst drought in Queensland" of 1992, and see how many stock died statewide, and how many were shot, not because of the shortage of grass, but because of their depreciated values. Maybe it's time to admit that droughts are not so much natural disasters as a part of nature's cycle — and that the only true disaster is the way people see the land solely in terms of money and how much they can make out of it.

There are many Aboriginal families with similar backgrounds to Ruby's, and many individual men and women with great personal stories to relate. It was not so much a matter of who to include in this book as who I must decide to leave out. As you have seen, I knew a little about Ruby and the country from which she came before I began to compile these histories. So here, for your interest and enjoyment, is the story of Ruby de Satge, musterers' and drovers' cook, boundary rider, housemaid, fencer and Jill of all trades in the bush. Working with travelling mobs of cattle from the vast Victoria River in the top end of the Northern Territory across Queensland into New South Wales, Ruby saw much more of outback Australia from the back of a horse than most of the white explorers.

Ruby now lives in Mt Isa. She is a short, dark woman, her fingers now partly curled from digging post holes in hard black ground with a crowbar, cutting gydgea posts with an axe, boring holes with brace and bit. One shoulder is troublesome as the result of hard falls from galloping horses; a scar beneath her right eye is the legacy of a mustering fall and a parting kick from the horse. Outside her house she walks with the aid of a stick, reminder of yet more dislocated and broken bones. She talks in a rapid, clear voice, sometimes almost too quick for recording, and her laughter comes spontaneous and clear as her eyes light up with a mischievous gleam.

Ruby remembers the good times in her life of wandering the stockroutes of the west, from the unfenced acres of Victoria River Downs in the top end across Queensland to Warren in New South Wales. And she remembers the bad times and the injustices of the past. Hers was a fight for equality and justice and independence, and I believe she certainly won that fight — no mean feat for an Aboriginal woman in the white male-dominated society of the time. Before women's rights became fashionable and laws were passed against discrimination in the workplace, Ruby had been there and done it all — simply because she disliked housework and being around town, and knew no better way of life.

Although Ruby could or would not tell me the year she was born, she said: "I can tell you exactly *where* I was born, four miles from Urandangi under a big old coolabah tree on the banks of the Georgina River. I was the second of eight children, six boys and two girls."

Her father was Thomas de Satge. Her mother, Janie, came from the Urandangi area. It was here and around Djarra that Ruby and her sister and brothers were brought up, moving from station to station wherever her father was employed as stockman or boundary rider. Thomas de Satge had a bit of education, which undoubtedly helped, back in those days, to keep the family together, since he was able to stand up for some rights. Janie de Satge had been taken away from her mother when she was a little girl and reared by others.

"No matter about the mothers," Ruby said. "That was one of the bad, really sad things about the past. A lot of bad things happened, and some lived to tell horror stories of injustices. At night, sitting around the campfire, they passed on these stories of inhumanity towards the children. So we were fortunate to have my father to protect us." Her face clouded as she told me: "Even young boys — the policeman come down and say, 'Roll your swag, you work for that fella'. And no matter if that fella bad man, you went to work for him — or else you went to the mission, or to gaol."

Injustices ...

Ruby recounted one incident that happened later on in her life. She spoke of her old friend Bubbler, who was employed on a station where she was working. The white head stockman wanted to teach him a lesson, so he walked up, punched Bubbler, knocked him over, then grabbed a shovel, intending to bash him with that. Bubbler, however, got up and in self-protection knocked whitey down, took the shovel off him and told him what he thought of him. The police were called and Bubbler was given three months' gaol in Stuart Creek. "When he come back," Ruby said, "people asked him: 'What you do in gaol?' — 'Oh brother, I been polish the taps, polish the taps all the time, polish bloody taps, all them taps that shiny you can see blackfella face in them!' " — This, I thought, highlighted the humour and laughter that could not be stifled even by such injustice. As it happened, years before I had worked with this same old man, Bubbler, and a more dignified and gentle man I had never met. I had not known this story at the time, and when Ruby related it to me, I wondered what would have been the outcome of that encounter if Bubbler, instead of defending himself, had laid on the ground and the arrogant white head stockman had hit him with the shovel and killed him. Would he have had to face a charge of murder? It's doubtful — such was the mentality of those times, when injustice combined with inhumanity to bring out the least favourable traits in human beings around the world, whatever their tribal clan, colour or religious belief.

Ruby remembers a carefree, happy childhood, never seeing the inside of a schoolroom, but sometimes waiting outside the schoolyard at the end of the day for her playmates, both black and white. "In them days," she said, "nobody worried if Aborigines went to school or not, so instead we learned to ride real young, going to bring back the horses hobbled out. But we would only bring half the mob back, and I still recall how my old grandfather would say 'Where them horses then?' And we would tell him: 'Oh, they off on the other track,' and away we'd go, riding past the lost horses, looking for kangaroo and emus — we'd chase them flat-out and off they would race, twisting and turning, trying to escape us half-wild Aboriginal kids riding our horses bareback, whooping and yackeyeing after them.

"How we escaped real injury or being killed I don't know, racing like that through the trees, over ant bed, stony hills and broken creek bank that was our unfenced schoolroom and playground. Sometimes we went bush with Dad in the wagonette, along with our horses and goats and underneath the wagonette, in a wire coop, our fowls. There was no shortage of eggs or milk and plenty of bush tucker and fish. We were on the move a lot until we went to Djarra in about 1938. I remember we took a mob of sheep to Fort William on agistment, Dad looking after them. A dingo was killing lots of sheep and the station owner says: 'If you catch that dingo I'll give you five pound.' So I copied what my father used to do, setting traps, and one day when we checked them, this big Alsation-dingo dog, a real killer, he was in the trap.

"My first job — I don't know how old I was, but I remember having to rise in the dark and then, carrying an old hurricane kerosene light, I'd walk across the creek to the local store, where I was paid ten bob a week to polish and scrub floors as a housemaid. It was no hardship, just a way of life I didn't enjoy."

So it was inevitable that one day, when a drover who was

short-handed came through Djarra and offered Ruby a job, she accepted it. By now she was an experienced rider, and she soon realised this was the life for her! Alas, the job did not last because of a bloke Ruby described as "a real jackaroo" and his reluctance to do his fair share of night watch around the cattle. Every night after Ruby had finished her two-hour watch she would try to waken this roo, but to no avail — he would not leave his swag. So since she was too small to kick him in the guts or tip him out of his swag, Ruby would end up doing half his watch as well. She complained to the Boss, who said: "Tie the night-horse rein to his arm or leg or his swag and just go to bed." But Ruby decided this was silly: if the night horse should take fright it would drag the jackaroo and his swag around the flat and what a terrible cattle rush there'd be! No night horse, no cattle — and no roo.

When they were passing through Boulia, Ruby met a friend who was looking for work, a real experienced drover. She said to the Boss: "I'm leaving — you know why. Billy gonna take my place." When the roo asked her "Why you leaving?" she told him: "I'm doing half your watch every night but not getting half your pay. I'm going, but you be careful of this fella that's taking my place. Don't stir this other Murrie up — he's a bad man, done time for murder. Once he raped a man in his swag after he wouldn't get up to do night watch."

Ruby began to laugh as she told me how, months later, she met Billy again and asked him how he'd got on with that roo. "Oh, he's a bloody good mate, that fella. Ya only gotta ride towards his swag at night and he'll be out of it even before you call out to wake him up!" Then Ruby told Billy the story she'd spun the roo, and they both had a good laugh.

This was how Ruby began the life of a stock worker on stations in this area, including Carandotta, once owned by Oscar de Satge. As we talked, she showed me documents relating to the de Satge mob.

In 1943, realising the importance of getting a fair wage for a fair day's work, she bought her first union ticket — it cost ten bob. With this, plus her willingness to speak out, she ensured that she received a decent wage.

Ruby suffered her first serious accident while she was working in a mustering camp — a dislocated shoulder. She did not seek medical treatment, and today she pays the price for that oversight. Her painful shoulder also helps her recall another incident that happened at that same mustering camp.

"We camped in the dry bed of a creek not far from a big tree called 'the hanging tree' and as we were riding out one day, the head stockman — he was Aboriginal — said: "Youse want to see where they hanged some Murrie?' — 'Bugger that,' I told him, but he led us past this tree, and pointed out a piece of wood a coupla feet long, sticking out from the tree fork. It must've been put there years before, because the tree had overgrown it. That piece of wood was supposed to have been used as a lever years before by white hunters when they hanged the Murries after their bullets had run out. That place was called Little Mossman. — And I remember that same night, in the dry bed of the stony creek where we camped, we found a lone pelican miles from water."

Ruby also became a boundary rider, moving stock from water to water in dry times. Her first long droving trip was from Victoria River Downs to Walgra Station with the Sowdens, a well-known droving family of the outback. Joe Sowden's wife travelled with him as cook.

"This was the life I grew to love," Ruby told me, "always on the move, seeing different people, different country. Riding around the herds at night was no hardship. Sometimes I helped with the cattle, sometimes with the Sowden children." The sun always rose bringing a brand new day and new adventures for Ruby and those kids, who grew up on the stockroutes, travelling with the cattle mobs until they were old enough for school.

"They were great people to work for, the Sowdens, and they took me with them wherever they went," Ruby said. "Like that time in New South Wales, after we'd delivered the cattle and were all going along to the picture show. When we got there the local Murries tell me: 'Blackfellas gotta sit down the front.' — 'Bugger that,' I said to Mrs Sowden, 'I won't stay to see the bloody show.' But she said: 'Come on, we'll all walk in together. If they bar you they'll bar us and we'll all walk out and get our money back.' — Well, I walked in with them, riding boots and all, and nothing more was said."

Ruby had more to say about travelling with the Sowdens. "I can't remember if it was my first or second trip with them — it was about 1952, when Mrs Sowden's daughter Glenda was born at an outstation on Victoria River Downs. We were mustering there a few months, bringing in wild cattle from the huge unfenced pastures. Sometimes I would go mustering, other times I would be cooking for the packhorse camp. Those cattle were like brumbies, real wild. As we got the mobs in hand they'd be sent off and we'd continue mustering. The stockmen were mainly Aboriginal, real smart they were. Though they hardly spoke any English they knew what was being said in the camp."

"Sad, that," I commented to Ruby. "It always seemed to be the Aborigine who was ready to listen to English and learn it, but the white people made no effort to understand what the Aborigines were saying."

Ruby recalled the Aboriginal families in that mustering camp. "Them little kids just this high" — she touched her knee — "they'd do a great job. There'd be eighty or ninety plant horses feeding out there on the flat, and then you'd see those other horses with saddles on, further out, circling around. You'd think, 'That's strange', then you'd see this little thing sticking up out of the saddle and you'd realise the Aboriginal kids were tailing those plant horses. They got no pay, not much food and plenty abuse — 'Come over here, ya black bastard, get over there, you so-and-so!' " Ruby imitated the harsh voice of a white boss.

"Sometimes I'd go to cook for the drovers' camp. The station camp had a dirty old white fella whose job was to cook for the Murri stockmen. After they arrived back from a hard day's work that old man would sing out: 'Come and get it, ya black so-and-so's!' and what they got was a fresh chunk of meat they had to cook for themselves, sometimes a damper, other times only flour, and then they had to set to and cook johnnie cake after ten, twelve or fourteen hours working. There were potatoes and onions going bad — that old white fella was too lazy to cook them.

"He used to come over to where I would be cooking for our camp, he'd sit on a log and watch everything. I would make lots of curry and stews, and custard and rice. I never asked that white fella to have a cup of tea in our camp, which was always the custom in the bush, because of my dislike for him and the way he treated the Murries. I would sing out to the little kids, tell them to come over and bring the men, then I'd give them cooked tucker — cold meat, custard, rice, open a few tins of fruit and they'd have a real big feed. And that white cook, he'd sit on his log and he says, 'You know the manager won't like you spoiling the blacks.' — 'You colour-blind or something?' I asked. 'They're black and I'm black.' — 'Well, the boss don't like your sort of blacks talking to them — you learn them about money, you learn them about food and wages and stuff.' — 'I'll talk to who I like.' — 'Well, the boss won't like it, putting silly ideas into their heads. You learning them bad habits.'

"Another time, when we were short of meat, I told them Murries as they rode into camp after a day's mustering: 'No meat! If you fellas want meat, get a killer — there's some quiet cattle around the water trough.' So them fellas let their horses go, had a drink of water, then took off their riding boots and went out to where those cattle were watering. Then they took off, running barefoot, catching a bullock by the tail and throwing it. — Gee, they could run, them fellas!"

I asked Ruby about the big wide scar under her right eye.

"I got that on Victoria River Downs. Out mustering we were, and them cattle was real wild. Most times you would only see a cloud of dust or hear timber cracking as you got near them. One day I took off after a mob with these local Aborigines, trying to turn some cattle back into the mob in hand. But my horse, which I had shod only the day before, fell as it turned. The kneepad was torn from the saddle. As the horse struggled to his feet, he kicked me under the eye. I was knocked unconscious. The men chasing the cattle saw what happened — they feared I'd been killed and came back. Later I learned that they went to a spring close by to fill their quartpots, then soaked their shirts and tried to revive me. When I did come to I was still knocked silly — I thought I'd fallen asleep on dinner camp and those fellas were playing games, waking me up to go back to work! 'What you doing?' I said. 'Leave me alone.' But they told me, 'You gotta go out-station and then to Darwin to get fixed up,' so I was escorted back to the out-station. By then my eyes were both closed and my face was swollen and blue. But I wouldn't go to Darwin, and for the next few weeks I stayed around the house with Mrs Sowden and her baby.

"One day we drove out to take rations to where the men had their dinner camp. When we reached a waterhole, I threw a fishing line into the water and left Mrs Sowden there as I walked back to the truck for something. Suddenly I heard these ungodly screams from Mrs Sowden. I thought, 'The baby's fallen into the waterhole!' and I turned to race back. Then, through my still half-closed eyes, I saw her racing towards me screaming, her baby under one arm and her little pommy dog under the other. 'What's wrong, what's wrong?' I yelled. — 'Big snake!' — 'Where?' — 'There!' she shouted — and not far behind was the biggest snake I have ever seen, coming straight towards me. 'Did it bite the baby or the dog?' I asked — 'No,' she said as she climbed onto the back of the truck, 'but he's still coming after us!' Even though my right eye was still half-closed, I got the .303 rifle out of the truck and climbed up onto the back. This huge snake was still coming, so I lay flat-out on the truck, took aim, fired — and got him!"

"That was the same year when we coming through the Murrinji Track," Ruby told me. "Oh, that's bad, just a graded track through this thick scrub. Sometimes cattle walk off into the bush and then you gotta get off your horse and walk around the straying stock to get them back into the mob. There's no room to ride a horse. The watering

places along its length, windmills and tanks, they miles
apart. One day, cattle stringing out along the narrow track,
I seen these things that looked like big red bumps on one
side. When I got up close I see they was little motor cars
with people inside them, pulled over to let the cattle pass.
They was competing in the Redex Trial that year and had
become lost or broken down, I don't know, but there they
were in the middle of the Murrinji, covered in red powdery
dust, just like bumps on the road.

"Another time, I don't know what year, after we passed
through the Murrinji we had to pick up a mob of stolen
cattle from Victoria River Downs. They were left at this
watering place and we put them into the mob. Someone
had already been tried and convicted of stealing them —
he tried to change the bull's head brand into something
else. I saw that fella later in Isa.

"One time I remember Mrs Sowden having to leave us
out on the Barkly Tablelands and drive herself to Mt Isa to
have another baby. The rest of us went on with the packhorse plant and I did the cooking. She was a great woman,
Mrs Sowden, droving all the time, having babies, coming
back and droving with the youngest while the others went
to school. They had only one child when I first went with
them, but eventually they had eight. To begin with their
transport was a rubber-tyred wagon drawn by three horses.
Later they got a truck. Mrs Sowden was a great cook, she'd
make bread every day, packing and unpacking the truck …

There were two old Aboriginal stockmen, they was with
the Sowdens longer than me. Bronc and Jerry Sowden, they
was known as, but they had Aboriginal names too. One
came from Booraloola way, the other from around Boulia.
They was the main actors in the team and they watched all

the Sowden kids grow up. Great stockmen they were, them two.

"We done a lot of trips together, sometimes we'd be working non-stop for months and months, don't ask me how long, I never worried about the days or weeks it took to drove cattle. One year we took a mob from Springvale down near Thargomindah, and then they had to go to Nappa Merrie Station to collect another mob and take them to Bourke, in New South Wales. Well, we couldn't get to Nappa Merrie, the Wilson River was flooded at Noccundra pub. So we waited on the eastern side and the station musterers swam them over to us — that was our first trip into New South Wales. At Hungerford, policemen counted the cattle through the big dog-netting dingo barrier fence into New South Wales, then we went to a watering place where you paid for the water — but at night you could have uninterrupted sleep with the cattle in the enclosure.

"When we got to the Darling River at Bourke, it was running real wide, and we had to pay to have quiet cows to lead them cattle over the big bridge. Gee, I remember that high, arched wooden bridge spanning the Darling River! Having come from further out, where the rivers weren't always full of water, it seemed strange here, the waters always running. I recall how the wooden decking of that big bridge would rattle and the cattle, frightened by the sound, would trot faster. Rising high from the middle of the bridge was a big steel structure. They told me this was used in flood time to raise the bridge decking and allow paddle steamers to pass upstream. Before the advent of trains, the country relied as much on river transport as on horse or bullock-drawn wagons. Another time at Bourke the river was low and we swam the cattle across.

"And I remember, once we took a mob from Springvale

and headed for Wodonga, in Victoria. That was another big trip, but we didn't get to Wodonga in the end, because when we reached New South Wales they told us we gotta deliver the cattle to Warren instead, near Haddon Rig — you know, that big sheep stud place. That was good droving, going into New South Wales, first them enclosures around the watering places and no night watches, then little narrow lanes for stockroutes. The cattle were all well broken-in by now, and we'd let them go at sundown. They would camp till dawn without needing any watching unless something unusual happened to make them rush. At all the farms people came out to talk to us. We got plenty of fresh eggs, fruit and vegies, sometimes trading beef for supplies. It was great seeing the different country, with wheat and other crops growing — unlike the mulga forests and stony plains of the Channel country, where you saw no one for weeks at a time. Down there in New South Wales you was never out of sight of houses or people.

"Well, when we'd finished that trip there we was in Warren, cleaning and washing on the creek bank one morning, getting ready to explore the town (this was the time the local Murries tell me: 'You gotta sit down the front' at the picture show), when up rode this common-ranger. Common-rangers were employed by most outback towns. They had to ensure that straying stock didn't annoy the townsfolk, control the number of stock each householder was allowed to run on crown land, and make sure mobs of travelling stock didn't loiter on the stockroutes and eat out the grass. Sometimes the drovers called them 'town sheriffs' when they tried to hurry them on. — Well, this old bloke, he's sitting on his horse and he says, 'You people shouldn't drink that water. Dead man's body in there.' Shortly after a woman found it caught in some tree roots not far away. I always remember that."

"That musta been a real eventful trip," I said to Ruby as she finished telling me about it.

"It lasted months and months," she said. "That's the time we went on to Sydney, too." She grinned as she recalled her visit to the big smoke. "After we'd been a few days in Warren, Jerry and Bronco started back for home with the packhorse plant, then the wagonette was loaded onto the train and we went with it and headed for Sydney. We stayed there a few days and I went to that big zoo a few times. I was fascinated by the animals and them big snakes in the cages, coiled up like big truck tyres. You weren't allowed to take pictures of them, but I did." At this point, Ruby rummaged through an old biscuit tin and showed me a faded photo of a huge rhinoceros. "I took that," she told me proudly. Then she began muttering about people who, over the years, had somehow reduced her cherished photograph collection. In those early days, she told me, she always carried an old box camera about. She just hoped that somehow those lost photos were preserved. So did I.

The next moment she laughed as she recalled the night in Sydney when she ventured out alone to a cinema not far from where they were staying, at the People's Palace. After the show she wandered around. She'd been sure she could find her way back, but she just couldn't find the Palace. Getting desperate, she spied a policeman standing outside a big building and in her rapid-fire speech she told him she was lost.

"He said, 'Come over here', and we walked across the street. Then he turned and said, 'Didn't you tell me you were staying at the People's Palace?' — 'Yes,' I said. — 'Well, look there,' he answered, and he pointed to this big building across the street, where we'd just come from. It had a name written across it and he began to read out the letters slowly and loudly: 'P-E-O-P-L-E ...' — 'What's that?' I asked. — 'It's the People's Palace!' he told me. — Gee, that was funny!" Ruby laughed heartily at the memory. "I'd been standing right in front of the place when I told the policeman I was lost! I felt real shamed, but I been laughing about it ever since."

After that they all caught the train back to Brisbane, travelled up to Townsville and then back to Djarra, a round trip of some thousands of miles.

Ruby told me something about her other work.

"Fencing was a real hard job, cutting gydgea posts with the axe, then loading them. But worst of all was digging post holes. That old crowbar would just ring out and your hands would jar as the point hit hidden stones when we dug. Sometimes my hands would be that blistered, I'd have to tie them up with handkerchiefs. In summer, out on the open plain, a crowbar left lying on the ground would be red hot when you picked it up. I did that work when I was still with the Sowdens after droving and mustering was finished for the year. We built fences and yards on Carandotta. Gee, boring holes in them gydgea post with brace and bit was hard!

"Sometimes I went boundary riding, shifting cattle from one watering place to another in the hot summer months and pumping water for the stock. I did lamb-marking, too, mustered the sheep for shearing and worked in the shearing shed at Carandotta. There were 50,000 sheep at Carandotta when I worked there as well as the cattle."

I recalled how, a hundred years ago, Oscar de Satge had

lost 90,000 sheep and 10,000 cattle from drought. Like so
many others before and after him, he regarded the country
solely as a place to make money, and grossly overstocked
the pastures. There are still people like him, who expect to
make money from the land without putting anything back
into it. The types of animals farmed in such huge, almost
plague proportions in marginal grazing areas are a disaster,
with their hard cloven hooves — sheep and cattle, as well
as the wild donkeys, goats and pigs, all imported to Australia
along with horses. Yet the native creatures with their flat,
soft padded feet so well adapted to the climate and the
landscape such as the roo, the emu — and the camel — are
treated like vermin. Are those who farm the hard-hooved
animals waiting for the land to adapt to them? Why not take
up large-scale farming of native animals? Unlike the white
Australians, the kangaroo was never the national emblem
of Aboriginal Australians — but it was always of prime
importance in their lives, supplying food, clothing, tools
and other things.

Ruby told me about a couple of other droving trips she
remembers well. On one of them she was heading into
Winton with a mob from Marion Downs. In the mob was a
cow with a long, bushy tail growing from the top of its neck.
"I took a photo, but it's one of those that have gone
missing," she said sadly.

   "There was another Aboriginal drover travelling behind
us on that trip," she went on, "and one day, near a certain
waterhole where a grave had been dug, he asked me: 'Did
you see the min-min light last night?' We'd only camped a
few miles apart, you see. — 'Gee, I was frightened,' he told
me. 'I couldn't sleep, I been riding around all night carry-

ing my gun.' Well, I knew he was trying to scare me, so I said: 'Yes, I seen that light when I was on watch — and you know what it was? It was a man carrying a torch, he got lost out on the plain. I talked with him and we shook hands. I shook hands with the min-min light!' — That drover, he rode off quick smart!" Ruby doubled over with mirth. "Yes," she told me, "I shook hands with the min-min light — or at least the man who was carrying it, not far from that waterhole and the un-named grave between Boulia and Winton, in western Queensland. The so-called birthplace of the mysterious, unexplained min-min light that every drover talks about.

"I never felt frightened alone in the bush," Ruby told me. "If I heard a strange sound or saw something strange, I'd just have to find out what it was.

"But I was scared of lightning as I rode around — there might be storms day or night, and sometimes when I was on night watch with the cattle I'd take extra socks and put them over the shiny stirrup irons.

"We had a couple of real bad cattle rushes. One was when we were taking cattle from Lake Nash to Djarra. We camped a few miles from Urandangi, and they was a real galloping mob when they rushed there. Gee, they galloped! I had just finished my watch and lay down in my swag. It was like a thunderclap when they rushed — deafening! I jumped onto an extra night horse and saw that one mob of cattle had split off, passing on one side of the camp, rushing so close that dirt was thrown up across the swag where Mrs Sowden slept with her baby in her arms. Eventually I managed to turn the leader and stop that mob, then held them for a while, settling them down and looking out for the glow of the campfire to tell me where I'd got to. Then I heard the others driving the cattle back to camp, and soon I saw that fire blazing. It was almost daylight by the time we got them all back."

"Everything was under control again after daylight, and then as the cattle were moved off camp we saw the aftermath of that rush. Some came limping and eight or nine head had broken legs or backs and were unable to move at all. They had been slow to jump up in that split second when the rush started. But things could have been much more tragic, for in the daylight we could plainly see where the rushing cattle had passed within a few feet of the swag where Mrs Sowden had been sleeping with her baby. It was covered in clods of dirt thrown up by the rushing cattle."

From my own experience I can attest to the almost indiscernible, chilling sound of the start of a cattle rush at night. Riding on watch, it is uncanny how whatever causes the rush can be transmitted in a split second through a resting, sleeping herd of a thousand head. A split second and they are suddenly on their feet galloping, those too slow to rise ending up lame or dead beneath the rushing hooves. That first explosion is something that has to be experienced to realise what it is like. Sometimes a cause can be found for the start of a rush, at other times there seems to be no reason.

"It may be," I said to Ruby, "that like humans, cattle have bad dreams — yet how could they be transmitted in a split second to all the others?"

Ruby told me that mob of cattle was about the worst she'd ever worked with. Even in daylight they'd sometimes take off, flat-out, and by the time they managed to stop them, their tongues would be hanging out.

Like many others in the dry seasons, Ruby sometimes cut

station fences to take horses off the stockroute to find grass
— a more or less accepted practice. It was, however, a crime
to use the paddock and then leave the fence wire on the
ground so that the station stock could wander.

Once, near Boulia, Ruby was watching some of the Sowdens' cattle close to the road when the station owner came
along swearing and cursing: another drover had let his
cattle go and they had walked up and down the black soil
dirt road in the rain and really ploughed it up. He got out
of his car and began to abuse all drovers. "He kept on
cursing," Ruby said, "and I kept nodding my head and told
him that another drover had left the fence wire undone. I
knew where he was too — drunk in the pub. Then the
owner looked real hard at me and exclaimed: 'Hey, you're
a woman!' and he jumped back into his car and took off. A
woman who worked for him told me later that he felt real
shamed when he realised he had been cursing and swearing
in front of a woman."

On another trip from Carandotta to Djarra, Ruby was
working for a drover called Billy Newman, who was travelling with his wife as cook and their two or three little kids.
Ruby's father was with them too — he was quite old by that
time. Soon after they started, real big rain came down in
the night, and by morning it was impossible to move the
old truck. (They had no packs.) So Ruby, her father and
another young stockman kept going with the horses and
cattle. "Boss gonna catch up later when the road's dried
out," Ruby told her dad.

But it rained all day. "Anyway, we had dinner at a station
called Calara, where the station manager come down and
he said: 'What you fellas gonna do, you got no swags, no
tucker, no packs. The cattle gotta be in Djarra for the

trucking date. I tell you what — you fellas go on tonight and I'll bring some swags and tucker to you.'

"So I went on night watch in the rain. I would be listening to the horse bells, to hear if they was walking away, and I'd wake the little white boy and tell him to watch the cattle while I brought the horse back. My dad was so old he couldn't see much at night, so it was no good him going on watch. That manager of Calara, he was real good to us, and next day we went on, and still Billy Newman never caught up with us, the road was that boggy. Well, we got them cattle to Djarra and the manager rang up with a message: 'You gotta cut out the fat cows from the bullocks and truck them yourself.'

"One of my brothers was in town, so I told him to come on down to help us do some drafting on the flat. Just as we were about to start, the Boss and his wife and the other kids turned up, so we got those cattle trucked on time — thanks to the help of the manager of Calara. That was a miserable wet trip, but it gave me a lot of satisfaction that we were able to do it on our own in time for the trucking date."

In the 1960s, Ruby went on her last droving trip. "I was in Djarra when Mr Sowden came through — his wife was living in Mt Isa by this time. Some of his kids were at school and a couple of the others were with him. He was short-handed and I went cooking for him. We took the cattle to Jessie Vale Station, left the droving plant there, and went back to Mt Isa in time for the big Rodeo. I recall the big bough shed with a roof made of spinifex where they served the grog — we got our drinks, then retired into the background, away from all them stockmen and miners waiting to be served, jostling and pushing ten deep, just like perishing cattle.

"Then, as we watched," Ruby recalled, "we saw smoke rising, and within seconds that spinifex roof was ablaze and there was a stampede away from the bar. I don't know how some missed being trampled." She told me how the fire was supposed to have started. It seems that one disgruntled stockman, unable to get close to the bar, had told his mates: 'I'll fix these bastards, I'll make some room around here!' Then he half-emptied the tobacco out of one of his tailor-made cigarettes, poked in some matches, stuffed back the loose tobacco, lit the cigarette, gave a couple of puffs, and threw it onto the spinifex roof. Woosh! The whole lot went up in seconds. I was amongst the crowd of thousands that attended the Mt Isa Rodeo that year, and I recall this incident. For years I've wondered whether that brainless idiot was caught. He certainly cleared a space around the bar, was he ever served his beer — and was he ever caught?"

After the Rodeo, Ruby returned with Mr Sowden and they took cattle from Lorraine Station to the other side of Camooweal.

That was the end of the eventful and rewarding droving life of one of the many unsung heroes of the pastoral industry, which but for this short account would remain untold.

Ruby told me that she worked mostly for good people, no really bad bosses — some just a bit cranky. Racism was a way of life in those days, but Ruby did not have any bad experiences around where she worked. She enjoyed equal pay and working conditions because she'd spoken out back in the early 1940s, buying her union ticket. "But down in New South Wales and in the Northern Territory the way they treated Aborigines was real bad. I've had a pretty good life, no regrets, I've seen Australia from horseback, enjoying the droving trips, I've had good times and bad times. Today people say to me, 'But you missed this and that, doing what you did,' but they don't understand. Being born in the bush we had our independence. And anyway, how you gonna miss something you never had?"

"How about comparing the way of life in those days and today?" I asked her.

Ruby replied without hesitation: "Them days was best, we might not have had much money but nearly everybody worked. Today they pay people who work, they pay people to go to school, they pay people not to work, and there are machines for everything."

Ruby's other achievement was to rear her sister's baby from the time she was a few months old. That baby, Elizabeth, is now a mother of two herself. As for Ruby de Satge, she is still independent, living alone and caring for herself. She is proud of her Aboriginal heritage, her contribution to the outback pastoral industry, and to the advancement of equality and justice for all.

Alf Barton

Restless spirits and a cultural cause

"What you been doing all your life?" I asked Alfie Barton, as we stood talking in the doorway of the Kalkadoon Tribal Council Museum and Keeping Place in Mt Isa, watching storm clouds gather over the rocky landscape that was once the tribal lands of the Kalkadoons. Today, the Dreaming Track beyond the door is the busy Barkly Highway, linking the whole east coast with northern, central and western Australia.

We watched the smoke rise from the huge smoke-stack at the rich copper and lead mines of the Isa, and as it drifted away I remarked how once there would have been only the smoke from cooking and hunting fires. Etched deep in the surrounding rocky hillside are ancient messages left long ago to warn passing countrymen. How was it possible for a so-called pagan, illiterate race to leave such messages, in a language thousands of years older than English as we know it today? Many of them are indecipherable now — there is a "communications gap". I spoke these thoughts to Alf.

"I know you are collecting material for a book about Aboriginal stockmen and women of the outback," he said. "So you are passing on communications and messages too." He paused. "During my lifetime I have had a lot to do with

communications. I spent twenty-one years working first for
the PMG department, then as a linesman for Telecom,
fixing overhead wires and laying underground cables. And
I'm proud to say that I also helped to install the first
solar-powered telephone transmitter, in the middle of
nowhere between Urandangi and Alice Springs. That was
my last job with Telecom, in fact."

Alf smiled as he told me: "Since I retired I've never
stopped working, mapping and recording ancient Aboriginal sites, keeping our culture and history alive. Unlike my
years with Telecom, this is an unpaid labour of love, recording the past after years of trying to shape the future through
understanding."

Alf is a spry man in his sixties. He has had two hip
replacement operations, yet he is fit and wiry-looking after
his years of hard work.

"You know," he said, "like most other young Aborigines
in the district, I also spent time as a stockman and drover.
This came about by accident — in fact, it was someone else's
accident that started my career as a ringer."

"Tell me more," I asked him, sensing that here was an
Aborigine who had made a real contribution to the history
of our land, and had a fascinating story to tell. When you
gather material for a book such as this, people far and wide
get to hear about the project. In different towns I would be
approached by well meaning folk who said, "You know old
So-and-so — he (or she) should be the ones you write about
and put in your book." Unfortunately, this book is just not
long enough and many people had to be left out. It would
in fact take hundreds of books to retell every story I have
heard.

But here, outside the Kalkadoon Tribal Council Museum, talking to Alfie Barton, I became more and more

interested in his story. His life, I realised, was one of rich fulfilment — and I sensed that he had faith that the future would prove better for everyone, whatever their colour, caste or creed.

"Well," said Alf, the "accidental stockman", "you know Quamby?" — I nodded. "Well, back in them days the train still ran from Cloncurry past Quamby onto Kajabbi and then Dobbin, where they trucked the ore brought in by camel teamsters from the rugged hills. One day I was there with some relations who worked on the railway line. And inside the pub were some stockmen who had their horses tied up out the back while they drank and tried to woo the local girls …"

Alf told me that one young white stockman, eager to impress the girls, went outside and mounted his horse, then began showing off his prowess, racing past the pub, wheeling and reefing his horse up and down the street, yackeyeing and whooping, flogging his horse with a battered old hat and always turning towards the pub to see if the girls were watching these feats of horsemanship. At last, flat-out, he raced towards the built-up area of the railway line — and arse-up went both horse and rider. The horse got up and stood waiting for that half-pissed galah to rise, but his yackeyeing and whooping had turned to cries of pain. His leg was broken, as the station owner and the others, including Alf, found out when they walked over to him. So the stockman was sent off to Cloncurry Hospital. At which point the boss turned to Alf and said: "You want a job?" — "Yeah," says Alf. — "Okay, you roll your swag, catch that horse and come out to my place."

— "And that," Alf told me, "was the accident that began my career as a stockman."

"But let's start at the beginning," I said. "Who were your people and when was you born?"

"I was born in 1931, in Cloncurry. My mother's name was Daisy. She was a Kalkadoon. Her mother was called Annie. She is mentioned in a book by Armstrong, who wrote that Daisy was her only child, but there were other children. Like others before and since, they were taken away, separated from their kinsfolk by station work or mission life. The mother of Alfie Clay, the great Aboriginal fighter of postwar years, was my mother's sister, and there were others, now being traced.

"My mother was a real fighter for Aboriginal rights," Alfie said proudly, "although she could neither read nor write. She was reared by white people who befriended my grandmother. Dad was a stockman and always away a lot. I had two older brothers, probably the last truly initiated members of the Kalkadoons. They were both taken away to work on a station when they were young, but I clearly remember this little old Aborigine coming to our home, and Mum telling me his name was Wild Harry, a survivor from the massacre at Battle Mountain. I was too young to understand it all at the time. I suppose his visit would have been something to do with my older brother's initiation.

"When we moved to Mt Isa we camped where the racecourse is now. Mum worked as a washerwoman, sometimes for the mines manager, who asked her to arrange a corroboree for them. Mum did this, and she also arranged trips for white and Aboriginal kids into the bush, passing on her culture and knowledge of the bush during these outings. This was in the 1940s — by then Mum had acquired a house. She also demanded of her local member of parliament that she be given the right to vote."

As I listened to Alf talk, I realised that here was a remarkable story of his mother's endeavour to arouse cultural awareness all those years ago.

"One thing I remember that will stay with me for ever," Alf continued, "is a sight I witnessed one time when Mum came home with these old men. She took us kids inside the house and said, 'Don't youse kids come outside'. But we could see through the holes in the tin walls, and we watched the people carry this crippled woman and lay her on the antbed ground. Then the old men began the ceremony, chanting and moving about. Well, we watched and soon that crippled woman sat up for a while, then she stood for a while, and finally she walked away. It was amazing, a miracle, I thought. I believe in the power of the spirits. They remain unseen and unexplained, yet when I visit certain places there is no mistaking the sensation of their presence in relation to certain sights. At those times I am aware of my relationship to the earth. That is why I believe it is important that we record and protect sacred sites and pass on to future generations their meaning and the stories relating to them."

It was during his childhood in Mt Isa that Alf first learned to fight for justice and equality. He recalled coming home from school one day and fighting five white kids who had ganged up on him. Suddenly an Irishwoman came out of a house and intervened, saying, "Give the poor bugger a fair go!" Then she turned to Alf and said, "Do you think you can beat these fellas in a fair fight?" — "Yeh," Alf replied. So the Irishwoman stood back and said, "Righto, you fellas, one at a time, see if you can belt him." Needless to say, after Alf had beaten the gamest three, the others decided to shake hands. "And you know," Alf told me at the end of this story, "we all been good mates ever since."

Alf's first job was working for a dairy, rounding up the

milking cows. He rode his bike the few miles to the farm each morning and afternoon. This was during World War II, and Alf recalled that either because of a shortage of rubber or lack of money, they couldn't afford tubes for his bike, so he had to chop up pieces of garden hose and use that as tubes.

During this period the Yanks moved in. The American military were going to commandeer the house Alf's mother had managed to buy — they wanted to use it as a warehouse for stores. But they didn't take into account the determination of Alf's mother, who approached the local government member and kicked up a big stink. So the house was shifted free of charge to its present location in Miles Street. That house still stands as testimony to an Aboriginal woman's determination to speak out and demand justice for herself and her people. It was about this time that Daisy Barton also demanded the right to vote, and was granted it.

It was after this first job as a real cowboy on a dairy that Alf became a stockman by accident. By now the war was over. I say "real" cowboy because, unlike the American cowboy, whose screen image shows him forever galloping flat-out on horseback shooting his gun, the Australian cowboy's job was to tend the milking cows and look after the fowls, the garden, and everything around the home-stead. The cowboy's boss was usually the missus, and most often he got to sleep in a bed each night — unlike the drover, whose bed was his swag, his bedroom wherever he camped each night with the swag rolled out on the ground.

It might be helpful to explain the differences between a drover and a stockman on the big sheep and cattle stations. The drover's job was to shift stock. He would move often-large numbers of cattle or sheep from one place to another, sometimes thousands of miles apart. In drought time he also walked stock to grass, or to the railway trucking yards to go to the meatworks, usually with horse-drawn wagons or packhorses, and later with motor transport. (This was before the advent of the road trains we know today.)

The job of the stockman or station hand was mainly to muster stock on the station, for branding or droving, and hand the cattle or sheep over to the drovers. Stockmen and station hands received the same wages, but the exact role of each has never been clearly defined, even by the courts. In the 1950s, stockmen across the country began to make a united effort towards standard wages and conditions, and the arbitration court handed down a decision that station hands should work forty hours a week, with penalty rates for Sundays, other holidays and overtime, and stockmen forty-four hours. But the judges weren't really able to distinguish between the two categories satisfactorily. Everyone on a station was known as a "stockman", and both stockmen and station hands sometimes had a break from the mustering camp and watching cattle at night, and got to sleep indoors in a bed with a mattress.

If all this sounds confusing, mixed up among the cowboys, drovers, station hands and stockmen were the jackaroos — privileged upper-class pastoral apprentices being trained, not really as stockmen but as future bosses. Then again there were the great stockmen who would never become great horsemen, and great horsemen who would never become great stockmen; the few who did were exceptional. Finally, don't get any of these categories mixed up with the bushmen: they were the ones able to find their way across trackless wastes of thick scrub and forest by day or night — they could read the land like a book. Aboriginal bushmen showed outstanding skill; to them it was a natural way of life. There were also white men who learned these

bushman's skills and became equally adept in understanding the land.

So much for all these different stockpersons — back now
to the story of Alf Barton. His first experience as stockman
on a station lasted a year, after which he had a number of
jobs, including one packhorse trip with cattle from Forest
Hill Station on the peninsula to just north of Hughendon.
After that he returned to Mt Isa, where he drove a bus for
a while. Then he became a truck driver, taking uranium ore
from a mine near Doomadgee Mission over 400 miles of
dirt track to Rum Jungle in the Northern Territory.

"Where did the uranium come from?" I asked Alf. And
I recalled one of my own droving trips in that area, when I
came across an abandoned uranium mine. Alf told me the
mine I had come across was indeed the same one he was
speaking about, a tunnel dug in the hillside of what is
known as the China Wall, a great rocky outcrop stretching
inland for many miles in that scarcely populated country
between Doomadgee and Borroloola in the Gulf of Carpentaria.

When I was shown that mine I recall staring at the stacked
pile of yellowcake outside the entrance and thinking — this
is the stuff powerful weapons are made of! It could be
mined by some mercenary with an eye for quick money, I
thought. All those years ago, surely it would have been easy
for some foreign power to mine that yellowcake, cart it the
short distance to the coast and ship it out of the country.
The authorities would have been none the wiser. — Maybe,
even in those days, I was starting to think like a writer, filing
away that uranium mine in my head as future material. But
now, years later, here was Alf Barton exploding my fantasy
about the illegal mining and export of uranium, for he was
the man who had in fact carted the ore away! Yet the picture

of that deserted mine and the stacked ore at the entrance has stayed with me, and I feel sure that one day I shall revisit that lonely but compelling part of the country again.

A forgotten uranium mine ... and Rum Jungle, once a name on everyone's lips, was also forgotten for years. But now both those sites are in the vicinity of new mineral development being planned, potentially worth billions.

After this, Alf worked for Fred Hird at Cliffdale Station, in the Gulf. That was wild, unfenced country full of clean-skin cattle. Most had to be thrown to be captured, and quiet cattle were used to get them to the holding yards. He also went droving with Fred, taking mobs from Lawnhill Station into Kajabbi trucking yards. From there, amid the ti-tree scrub and saltpans along the coast, intersected by idyllic freshwater lagoons, they would venture over the ancient eroded hills, where some of the world's most remarkable rock fossils are found, or onto the open rolling downs of the Barkly Tableland, and take cattle into Djarra, another busy trucking centre.

Alf told me about another incident in his life which happened in that country, at the famous Brunette Downs races. He walked up to the bar and asked for a drink, only to be told: "We don't serve blacks." He remained standing at the bar, determined to be served. A white drinker standing close by said: "You heard what the man said, piss off, you black bastard!" Needless to say, a fight ensued and Alf belted the piss out of that uppity white, then walked back to the bar and was served. He took no great delight in being able to beat racist whites, but he did prove that he was the equal of any.

"Such incidents and worse forms of racism were normal behaviour by white Australians at that time," he commented. "Even the non-payment of wages to top Aboriginal stockmen, while useless whites with no experience would receive full pay. The same went for our people under mission control."

As I have seen in my travels, "Ignorance combined with arrogance is the lowest virtue in any race." Sadly, it manifests itself in all peoples, even the Aboriginal race. Alf stressed that in those days, racism and injustices against Aborigines were bloody terrible.

"What about attitudes today?" I asked him. "Has anything improved?"

"Oh, improved out of sight. We can all walk in and get served our grog today — too bloody much, in fact. There are great work opportunities, education opportunities that were unheard of even twenty years ago, and for the first time we are being paid to record and keep alive our culture. We can all look forward to a great future."

Alf joined the PMG department in the early 1960s, but left soon after for a big money job at Mt Isa mines. "That was a good job," he said, "but I couldn't stand the fumes, so I left and was given another start by the PMG. And I stayed employed as a linesman operator for the next twenty-odd years." It was a job that took him and the gangs he worked with from Townsville to the Northern Territory border, into the Gulf and the Channel country of far south-west Queensland.

At first they installed and repaired the now almost obsolete overhead telephone lines, camping out most of the time. Over the years Alf witnessed the change from lines to underground cables. His last assignment, as he had said, was helping to erect a solar-powered transmitter in the middle of nowhere, between Urandangi and Harts Range in the Northern Territory, on the Plenty Highway. He is proud of the fact that he helped to install and maintain telecommunication over a vast area of outback Queensland.

Alf is equally proud of his new role in retirement. As he says, he is still involved in communications. He translates for tourists and anyone else who is interested the meaning of those messages inscribed on rock surfaces thousands of years ago, and of cave paintings. As we talked, we both realised that ages before the advent of the PMG and Telecom, Aboriginal Australia had its own means of keeping in touch. Now the smoke of the ancient signal fires has vanished, carried away on the winds of time, and the message sticks have crumbled and rotted and returned to the earth from which they came. But the engravings on the rock surfaces and the cave paintings are as important today as they were when they were first inscribed, thousands of years ago.

"You know," said Alf, "the Chinese and Afghans done a lot to help open up this country." He waved one arm, encompassing the city and its surrounding hills. "For years they worked around here, some of them mining gold and copper."

I nodded. The Afghans and their camel teams did much to open up the isolated mines, inaccessible by horse or bullock wagon. For, unlike other migrants, they were ready-made bushmen. "Maybe things would have been very different if the Afghans and the Chinese had been allowed to take up pastoral leases," I suggested. "But of course land rights were reserved exclusively for white migrants, most of them British."

I realised that from the time the first shipment of Afghans with their camels arrived in Melbourne in the 1860s, to help in exploration and later with transportation, they, like other dark-skinned migrants, would have suffered injustices. And because the camel teams were faster and cheaper than horse or bullock wagons, they aroused the resentment of the white carriers and did them out of work. Yet despite anti-Afghan sentiment, especially on the part of the transport union, the Afghans, like the Aborigines, survived. Finally motor transport took over and the Afghan drivers with their camels retreated into the ranges, helping to carry ore from Mt Isa mines to Duchess and Cloncurry — but that too ceased when the railway was extended to Mt Isa, in 1929. Many of the camel teams were not owned by their drivers, but were leased out to them by others who bred the camels at Bourke, in New South Wales. In the end the camels were turned loose to roam the land they had helped to open up. In 1942, one of the last loads of ore to be transported by camel train was trucked at Dobbin. A few wild camels still roam the ranges — today, alas, they are treated as vermin by many.

With these thoughts passing through my mind, I said to Alf: "Why didn't they run thousands of camels on the stations for their meat, milk and hides? The round flat pad of the camel, like those of the roo and emu, is ideally adapted to this inland country. Camels mostly browse the trees and bush tops, so to have experimented with running camels, emus and roos on the land would have cost very little. But no — instead, the land is ruined by the destructive cloven hooves of sheep, cattle and horses. And just think of the quantitites of poisonous chemicals that were used to keep those cloven-hoofed animals alive! Yet I have never seen a roo, an emu or a camel that needed to be dipped in order to keep it healthy. And think how much less soil erosion there would have been in these marginal grazing areas."

Well, so much for what might have been. Let's hope the

future will be shaped by people with vision, able to look two hundred years ahead and learn from the mistakes of the past two hundred years. I believe Australia is now the only nation in the world with the ability to record the past truthfully before it is too late. Before it is lost. The history of other nations is shrouded in mystery, myth and propaganda. But only if all of us tell the truth about our past.

Delma Barton, Alf's wife, is employed as Administrator of the Kalkadoon Tribal Council Museum and Keeping Place. She is also a singer and a didjeridoo player — and I can attest to the unique and haunting sounds she extracts from that traditional instrument. When I talked to Delma, she stressed to me the importance of education and culture. As a child living in an outback country town, she grew up with a feeling of inferiority.

"Even though we had qualifications, all the good jobs went to whites, whether they were qualified or not. It would be interesting to examine the old school records," she remarked. "Growing up, we were ostracised and suffered prejudice in many different ways. As a child, because of my unique voice and my interest in singing opera, I was ridiculed by both blacks and whites. In those days, developing talent in Aboriginal students was discouraged by all but a very few teachers. Aborigines were supposed to sing hillbilly songs and corroboree. Operatic songs became a taboo for me. But I went on practising by myself in the backyard, my only audience my family and the animals and birds." She smiled. "Today, I am putting together my own songs that come from Dreamtime inspiration."

She told me that she first learned to play and perform on the didjeridoo in 1985. The didjeridoo was supposed to be taboo for women players, but the one Delma plays was given to her and her young son, William, who also plays it, by tribal elders, and she plays it with their approval. Thus another myth is exploded — for here is a woman playing a didjeridoo with the complete approval of the elders who made it and presented it to her.

Delma told me that she has never studied music formally and does not write down the notation for her songs. She claims that the inspiration for her best work comes when she visits Aboriginal sites with Alf. "Something happens to me; I hear and compose the words and music in my head then and there, and file them away in my memory to perform later on."

Aboriginal culture and history have not been well documented to date. Nor have the achievements of individual Aborigines. Delma hopes that may soon change. She has just appeared in a documentary video featuring ten uniquely Australian characters, which has been sent to the British Tourism Commission, and may, perhaps, gain wider overseas distribution. Like Alf himself and young William, Delma does much to foster goodwill between different races while keeping alive her own Aboriginal culture.

One thing she is emphatic about is that amid all the talk of reconciliation between white and black, before that can succeed there must be reonciliation between all us Aborigines. I wholeheartedly agree with her.

The extra stories you hear while you are recording someone's life are often worth writing down. While I talked to Alf and Delma, another white-haired Aborigine, Cyril Chapman, came up and joined us.

Cyril was born of Coolallah Station, in Kalkadoon territory, on the Leichhardt River, about 1916. As we chatted, he told us how he was tracing his tribal ties with the past. Now in retirement after a hard working life, Cyril told us of good times as well as bad. He had suffered a great deal from bigoted views and oppressive, unjust laws. Like many others, he had been rounded up and sent to Palm Island. That is a truly black mark on white Australian history. Yet Cyril recalled an incident which, in spite of everything, showed that these deportees did not lose their spirit.

After he had been on Palm Island a while, a clergyman asked him and his brothers to come to church. If they did, he said, "The Lord will care for you." To which Cyril replied: "You get me off this filthy island and I'll look after meself." Needless to say, after this Cyril was marked out as a trouble-maker and a stirrer.

He recounted another story from his years on Palm Island. During the war, there were army and naval personnel on the island, and a ship was anchored there. For days, the Aborigines observed the periscope of a submarine rising from the ocean depths and cruising offshore. By the time they realised this was the enemy and the naval force prepared for action, the Jap submarine was gone.

Another time, a high-ranking naval officer came ashore and saw Australian soldiers guarding Aboriginal workers undergoing punishment. The officer asked the guard: "Hey, what's this? I've never seen black Jap prisoners before, how did they get here?" — "These ain't Japs, sir," the guard replied, "they're Aborigines." — "What!" shouted the top brass. "We're not fighting a bloody war with the Aborigines, we're fighting a war with the bloody Japs!" So the black Aboriginal prisoners were set free, and after that any punishment given out by the mission administrators was no concern of the defence force.

Later moved to another mission, Cyril fought with his so-called superiors and was expelled from the mission. "Yeh," he said. "I was sent to the mission, told to pray and let meself be taken care of, then after years of internment I was set free because I had this bloody great fight. After that I spent twenty years as an employee for Cloncurry Town Council, then I retired."

I recalled that during my stockman days, I had in fact met Cyril in Cloncurry.

When Cyril retired, he headed south to a former mission, now known as an Aboriginal community, where he lives surrounded by relatives, and sometimes makes visits to Kalkadoon territory.

Resuming my conversation with Alf Barton, he told me that he had seen great changes in his lifetime in attitudes towards our people. In earlier days, things were real bad — it almost seemed that in the eyes of the whites, it was a crime to be Aboriginal. Alf thinks it is the outlook and behaviour of past days which causes the tensions of today, and situations where young black people get into trouble.

"We need an Aboriginal station or training centre, where young people could be taken out into the bush and trained as labourers or stockmen or women. Not everyone can go to university or to work in an office and live on the coast, like white Australians," he said. "You know, I get some people here from Community Service who are good workers once they get going, but they don't have a real chance in life — they don't know where they've come from or where they're going. I would like to see our people's education covering everything, past, present and future, without losing the understanding of our culture or awareness of our identity."

Alf sees education as one of the keys to tolerance and understanding between peoples. He would like to see many more Aborigines become archaeologists or geologists. We both agreed that the charting of our history from the distant past to the present is too important to be entrusted to others, without input from Aborigines themselves.

Our talk turned to spiritual matters. Alf has seen the mystery of the pointed bone, and song ceremonies performed over people to undo evil curses. And he recalled one time when a couple of white stockmen came across a sacred site and took photographs. They showed these to another stockman, deriding the significance of the site and Aboriginal lore. Yet those same two stockmen would call foul if Aborigines questioned their beliefs of angels flying around and the miracles related in the Bible. Well, they showed the photos to this other bloke and laughed when he tore them up, saying they could be punished for their actions. But next day one of the stockmen had his leg badly broken and the other became violently ill, and only recovered after an old Aborigine treated him with bush medicine.

As a boy, Alf had seen a cripple get up and walk away after ceremonies had been performed. And one night he saw the mysterious min-min light, shining into a clump of trees hundreds of miles from anywhere, like a bright torch light. Yet when he went out to investigate next day, there were no tracks — nothing to explain it. On another occasion, he and Delma had pulled off the road and set up camp, but, tired as they both were, neither could sleep because of the eerie sounds and atmosphere around them. They sensed something beyond their control. They got up and moved camp, and slept soundly for the rest of the night. Next morning, they felt compelled to investigate their first camp, and discovered it was an ancient Aboriginal burial ground.

"There are some things you can't mess about with," Alf emphasised. "I believe in the restless spirits of the Dreamtime who are often able to avenge evil happenings."

"It's really very like Christian teaching," I remarked, to which Alf agreed.

"You know," he said, "we get a lot of visitors to this Kalkadoon tribal Keeping Place and Museum, and people who are interested in Aboriginal culture wanting to see significant sites in the hills. Some of those are still not open to the general public, of course."

"What sort of people do you get?" I asked.

"Oh, people of all nationalities and from all walks of life. More overseas people than Australians — it is only now that white Australians are starting to acknowledge that history in Australia did not begin with the First Fleet, but flourished tens of thousands of years before the Bible was written. Only now are they realising the significance of Aboriginal culture."

Later we climbed into the hills and I looked at a slab of rock that Alf pointed out to me. He transcribed the message etched deeply in its weathered surface, left thousands of years ago by his ancestors.

"You could say that I've turned my back on the present to help people understand the past and secure a better future," he said.

How ironic, I thought, that Alf Barton's final job for Telecom should have been to erect a solar transmitter in the desert. Today, he is busy transmitting by word of mouth messages and stories from the far distant past, embedded in the rocks and on the walls of caves.

Peter Hood

Polo, the gold cup and the night the Kuhn-kee called

Peter Hood was born near Thargomindah about 10th June, 1902, in a tin house with a dirt floor owned by a white family. It stood on a stony hill not far from an almost boiling-hot artesian bore. That bore would have some claim to fame, being the first to supply water that drove the generators to provide electricity for the town.

Thinking back to childhood days, Peter recalls that his favourite pastime was throwing stones — he used to pelt the other kids, both black and white, "simply because the stones were everywhere," he told me. He also recalls going with his mother to Thargomindah Station, helping her tend the garden, fetching the milking cow and chasing the fowls.

"Later on Mum was employed at Thargo police station and we lived there," he told me. "There was a police tracker there then." One day an Indian hawker pulled up down the flat, selling his wares to the whites and Aborigines who had come into town for the races. "In them days Aborigines weren't allowed to purchase grog, and these two gungies (policemen) watched through a telescope as the hawker sold an old Murrie a bottle of rum. So they saddles up their horses and gallops down. 'We're gonna pinch you, selling grog to them blacks.' — 'But I never sold no grog,' the Indian hawker pleaded. — 'We been watching you from the police station with a telescope,' they told him."

"How old were you then?" I asked Peter.

"Blowed if I know — but I was old enough to ride a bloody horse. I first learned to ride when we lived there at the police station. The first horse I got on was a big, stinking thing. I had no riding boots, only sandshoes."

"And how did you feel about that first ride?"

"Oh, it was a good feeling riding a horse, real good ..."

Getting up on that big, stinking horse was the beginning of Peter Hood's life in the pastoral industry — as a top-class stockman and drover, all-round horseman, rouseabout and polo player. He is also a husband, father, grandfather and great-grandfather. We talked at his grand-daughter Cindy's place, surrounded by his great-grandchildren and great-great grandchildren. Peter's story includes hardships, sometimes injustice, but also rewards and satisfaction in his work, his family life, and the many friendships he developed along the way. Like most great horsemen, Peter was reluctant to speak of his achievements, but he was willing to sit back and remember life in the outback from the time he first went to work — for Sir Sidney Kidman, on Norley Station.

"I was still a kid when Mum went to Norley. A police sergeant from Thargo took us out in a sulky. We lived in quarters near the homestead. Other Murries camped down the creek, some with their families. They was a big mob there. Some worked on Norley, others didn't. We never moved down to the camp. Every year they used to go to Noccundra races — Murries on horseback, packhorse, in buggies, sulkies and spring carts. Mum and I always stayed at home. Some got their tucker from the station — sugar, tea and flour. Others would go to the police station in Thargo to collect their money."

In them days of total oppression, most Aboriginal money earned as wages was paid to a "Protector", usually the local policeman, and there is no doubt that some Protectors made money on the side. Most Aboriginal workers were unable to read or write. Up to the Protector they would go. "What you want — money, hey? Okay, sign your cross here — oh look, you been spell him wrong, sign this new one" — and so two withdrawal slips were made out, but only one sum of money was paid. Right up to the present time there is a dispute concerning accumulated Aboriginal workers' wages entrusted to the Queensland government, totalling millions of dollars that disappeared.

The clan elders carried out ceremonies of initiation and renewal of their kinship with the land, and administered tribal law. These ceremonies were ridiculed by the white tribe that sat in church and worshipped an invisible god, waiting for chubby-faced angels to appear. What a sight it would have been in the Australian outback if that had ever come to pass: the clash of eagles and angels for control of the Australian sky. The old wedgetail is still present, though in ever decreasing numbers, and flying kangaroos leap across the continent, but there is still no sign of the angels.

I spoke of this to Peter, who laughed. He remarked that pigs could fly, if you put them in an aeroplane.

We got to talking about his work and wages on Norley, and how he progressed from riding in sandshoes to his first pair of riding boots. Like all the others at that time, Peter received very little money. But, he told me, they had no real need of money — there was nowhere to spend it. And each year all the stockmen were issued with riding boots, two shirts, trousers, a hat and blankets.

"We got two bob when we went off to Thargomindah races each year," he told me. "We'd saddle up our horses and ride about eighteen miles into town and be home again that night. Next day the same — another two bob, ride in and come home. Some of the others went in and camped along the river bank at Thargomindah."

"Well, that two bob each day would have been a bonus," I commented.

"Yeah, you could call it a bonus. For us it was the only time we saw any money."

"Didn't you ever see a statement of wages?" I asked.

"No, never seen no bloody statements," Peter said. "We just knew it went from three to five bob a week, then ten bob. Old J.L. Watts was the manager in those days — he was also the boss of Bulloo Downs. We all had to go to him to get our wages."

Peter told me that in all the years he was on Norley, he never had a buster.

"How come?" I asked, sceptical of this boast. I thought that anyone learning to ride bucking or bolting horses would have at least a couple of busters along the way unless they always rode quiet horses.

"Well," Peter said, "when I was learning to ride in the mustering camp, there was always some mongrel bolting buckjumpers there, but them old Murries would get on anything that bucked or was real bad. They was real good horsemen."

He told me that in the old days, rations used to come from Quilpie or Cunnamulla with horse or bullock teams. "Then old fella Kidman organised the Afghans to bring tucker from Adelaide on their camel trains — they was a lot faster than the horse and bullock teams." He laughed. "One time them Afghans found all this pork and bacon on their camels and chucked the lot to the shithouse."

I asked Peter how many men there used to be in the mustering camp.

"Oh, about six or seven whites and fourteen, fifteen Murries and the head stockman," he replied. "All of them white fellas used to help themselves to the tucker, but the Murries used to have theirs cut off. They was allowed to fill their quartpots with tea, and go to the table to get sugar, that was all. Well, them Murries, they'd watch the white man get out his swag in the morning, go and have a piss, then not even wash before he'd be there at the table, handling the tucker the Murries had to eat. Then one of the old Murries would get up and go to the head stockman. 'That man dirty, he never washed himself,' he'd say. So then the head stockman would tell that white man, 'Go and have a wash, ya dirty bastard, before you handle the tucker.'

"One time, that head stockman, Doug Houghton, chipped this bloke who'd come from another station — he never used to wash, and Doug told him to wash before he handled the tucker. Well, it turned out he was a station owner. — Yeah, we got him chipped, the dirty bastard." Peter laughed gleefully as he recalled this incident.

"That's how it used to be," he went on, "the dirty un-washed whites were allowed to handle the tucker and help themselves, and the Murries who was clean weren't allowed to get their own tucker."

"Maybe them whites thought the black on our skin would wipe off on the tucker like dirt and grime," I suggested.

Peter chuckled. "That's right!"

Being a lot younger than Peter, I did not experience this problem in south-west Queensland. Although stockmen and managers, bosses and jackaroos ate at separate tables at the station homesteads, out in the mustering camps everyone helped themselves. Standing by the open fire leaning on a shovel handle, the mustering cook would watch who washed and chip those who didn't. For around the campfire was the cook's domain.

"Then of course there were dirty cooks in some of the camps," Peter said. "There was one he told off, who used to cut bread or damper for the Murries holding it pressed against his chest and filthy shirt. Well, he didn't last long."

I recalled my own feelings when I worked up north and saw tucker being cut off in the mustering camps for the mission Murries. The old cook there said to me, "I told them fellas, if they wash they can cut their own tucker any time, but they don't want that, they happy as it is. Go and ask them if you like." This I did, and they told me they preferred sitting at their own fire, separate from the main camp and the others.

"I recall, too, one big station in the Gulf country. Here, when the mustering camp was at the homestead, the jackaroos ate at the big house with the boss and all the other workers, some Aboriginal, some not, ate at a big separate table. And in the room next door sat all them people from the missions, some great stockmen and workers amongst them. There was a big Aboriginal woman doing the cooking — she was a great cook, too.

"This is all wrong, I complained to her, "these fellas eating separately — they're the equal if not better than me as stockmen." The cook then informed me that she herself had voiced the same opinion many times, and had told all them people to eat where they wanted in her kitchen. For, like the domain of the musterer's cook, the homestead kitchen was the realm of the station cook — as many a stockman, jackaroo, manager, even station owner, has discovered. Well, this cook also told me it was their choice to eat separately from the others, and when I asked them, they confirmed her words.

So far as owners and managers were concerned, eating separately at the homestead was the accepted thing. I recall the time I was employed on a small station in the Rockhampton area. The manager was an old fella, thin as a matchstick, about five feet tall. His wife was short and three axe-handles across the arse. Also employed on the station was the manager's brother. He and I shared sleeping quarters away from the house and we got on good together. I got on good with the manager and his wife as well and she was a reasonably good cook. But at mealtimes when the bell rang, me and the other bloke would go up to the house, and there on the veranda would be two tables, one very small. The owner, his wife and brother would sit at the larger table, and not six feet away, sitting at my own private table, would be me. But I never once felt offended or inferior sitting there, and sometimes being asked rather unintelligent questions — their conversation was mostly based on headlines from *Country Life*. I was privileged I did not have to sit at the table. At night I would gulp down my food and dash back to listen to the radio. While I never once felt inferior to these narrow-minded people, I did not feel superior either; I realised that if I had, I would be no better than them. Besides, I knew from experience there were in fact uppity Murries as well as whites.

"Did you used to see plenty of bucking horses in the mornings?" I asked with a grin.

"I seen a few buck and throw the saddle — mostly white fellas, you know," Peter chuckled. "There was plenty of horses in the camp, over a hundred, and three horse-tailers,

all Murries. No paddocks out there, and mobs of brumbies —
I don't think them horse-tailers ever got to sleep. They were
good stockmen too, them old fellas in the mustering camp."

"Oh yeh, what were their names?" I asked.

"Oh, Jesus Christ! They're probably all dead now." Peter
mentioned some names that were familiar to me — I'd met
some of those old men as a kid. I imagined them riding like
mystical heroes, some in tribal dress, others in stockmen's
clothing, riding across the misty landscape of time.

"Yeh, they'd all be dead now, poor old buggers. They was
good men," Peter said, lost in memory. I imagined him
trying to conjure up dim, dark faces and the almost forgotten names of Aboriginal stockmen of the past, riding
against a background of stony ridges, mulga scrub, lignum
swamp, coolabah trees, gudgea and red dust. They left a
legacy of the stockman tradition, but their individual names
and deeds, such as those I am now recording, are lost and
gone.

"In them days," Peter went on, "there was only bronco
horses, no yards for drafting and cutting out cattle on the
open flat."

"How many cattle?" I asked.

"Oh shit, thousands and thousands and thousands.
When mustering started you would only get to see the
station from four or five miles away. Them blokes with wives,
they'd ask the boss: 'Go in tonight, see wife, ride back by
daylight?'

"There was about forty Murries camped at Norley then.
Four were employed full-time as woodcutters for the station.
There was a Chinese gardener, too, and a big vegetable
garden, but in the mustering camp you never saw one of them
bloody cabbages or tomatoes and other things grown there.
But we had plenty of potatoes, onions, damper and meat."

I nodded. Like the Aborigines, whose land was the basis of pastoral wealth, the contribution of the Chinese to pastoral Australia has not been sufficiently acknowledged. Mostly underpaid, they grew vegetables for the stations and towns of the inland and often cooked in the homesteads — for white pastoralists whose agenda was the amassing of wealth and power.

Peter was still remembering the mustering camps. "One time we were out in camp and we got plenty of duck and emu eggs. Them fellas, they had emu eggs in their saddle-bags, in their coat pockets, even carried them in their hats while they tailed the cattle. Well, one day I called out: 'Hey, Cuckoo!' — that was Alf's brother — 'there's a bullock back there!' and he started cantering back and all his bloody eggs smashed. He had these emu eggs in his saddle-bag and in his shirt, and the bastards smashed all over him when he started galloping." Peter laughed at the memory. "Oh Christ, but you couldn't laugh then, he was the boss, and in them days he would crack you double with the stockwhip.

"Another time, this Nockatunga Murrie and me were tailing cattle when he seen a goanna, and he chased and caught the bastard. Back at the camp he cooked it and was eating it for dinner when the boss came along. He went crook. He said, 'You can eat them bastards out in the bush, but not in my bloody camp!' "

Such was the ignorance of whites in those days. Here were people who had survived, unaided by whites, since the dawning of the dreamtime, free of diseases such as diabetes, whose survival can only be attributed to eating native food.

"In 1927 I went to Tobermary to work," Peter told me, "We had about 17,000 bloody sheep. That station belonged to the Watts. We fenced in the whole 722 miles of the bloody place. That was in 1932. We carted every post and bored them all, no bloody worries, done it with a brace and bit, crowbar and shovel. Yeah, and we done dog-netting fences too. There was only the Watts family and a few Murries, and that fencing took a long time.

"And don't ask me about the woolshed: it took me a day and a half to dig one bloody post-hole, nearly six foot deep they were. We built the woolshed and everything. I helped nail every frigging board in that shed, and every bloody piece of roofing iron. It was all bush timber.

"After I'd been at Tobermary six years, them old tribal kings gave me my wife, Janie. She was at Tobermary at first, then she went away to Comonagin with her aunty and her uncle, old Charlie Finch. They came round in a sulky and told me to go and get her, so I borrowed a horse off Watts, then away I went, taking short-cuts then straight up the bloody river, about seventy mile. I was a cunning bloke then. We was married then and come back together past Congie Station — my mother was there. Then we went on to Tobermary."

"How did you get your wife — did you pick her out, or did them old fellas choose her for you?" I asked.

"They gave her to me," Peter said. "They tell me, 'that proper one'. Yeah — you couldn't go and take whatever one you liked in those days."

"But you knew her beforehand?" I asked.

"Oh shit, you see I wanted another one, my wife's aunty, but they wouldn't give her to me, see. That was at Norley Station. Her mother and father wanted to give that other one to me, but them old Murries were all against it. Yet a few years later they turned around and gave me her 'lation — same meat, all the same blood. Topsy was the one I was going for, but they gave me her niece Janie, and so I took her."

"Who told you that you could have that one?"

"They came in a horse and buggy, that's when I got her. The old king from South Comonigin and old Bismarck, they came. Old Monica would be the only one of that whole mob alive still."

"How long did you wait to get a wife?"

"Bloody years after I left Norley. I didn't get her till I was thirty-four or thirty-five. A few years after we got back to Tobermary, this preacher came out that way to take services, and he married us the white way. Old Mrs Watts gave Janie away. Our daughter Pat was there, and Billy Clayton. After we got married I had to take Billy Clayton and the priest back to Norley Station."

"How come you couldn't marry the one you wanted — why didn't you run off with her?"

"Oh shit, no hope of that. They woulda got me. In those days if you got married wrong they'd catch you, and then one of you gotta die — see, that was the law."

The mention of death reminded Peter of a very bad time in his life. "It happened when we went to Eromanga races, where us Murries camped close together on the creek. It was winter and really cold. We kept a big fire stoked up in the middle of the camp, and there was a large billy-can by the side of the fire, with hot water for tea and coffee. It had a big tin plate on top of it. Janie, my mother and stepfather and my brother was all there with me.

"Well, when them races finished there was a dance night, and some of them Murries went up to watch the dancing, including my stepfather. (Aborigines, of course, weren't welcome inside.) Back in the camp, my mother and me were talking in the tent when we heard this noise from the fire when that tin plate sitting on top of the billy-can fell off with a loud clatter. There was no wind that night — it was real still. 'Something's wrong!' Mum and I both exclaimed fearfully. — 'Yes, Kuhn-kee Kuhn-kee,' I said — and it was Kuhn-kee all right, for at that moment my stepfather been killed.

"Next minute, one of them Murries came running down the flat, crying out. He told us what happened — our old fella been killed and his body stuffed into the boot of a car. All the Murries there had seen what happened. I went straight up to the dance hall and said to the policeman there: 'Where's the bloody fella that killed my stepfather?' — 'How you know about it?' he asked. He never told me anything. I got a bottle of rum from the pub and some sherry for my mother and the other women. They was all crying when I got back to camp.

"That was the greatest injustice I ever experienced, a very bad thing they done. When they held the hearing about the death, no Aborigines were allowed into the courthouse — but they all seen what happened, they seen my stepfather killed. And all them fellas said the man who did it should have been gaoled, but you see he was friendly with the police. But I believe he suffered later on in other ways."

In those days, squatters not only controlled local government but had influence over the courts and police affairs as well. The JPs and magistrates were their friends and relations.

As for that tin plate falling off the billy-can on such a still night for no apparent reason, maybe it could be explained scientifically. But to an Aborigine there was only one explanation: it was a message from the spirits. Kuhn-kee. The minute it happened they knew something bad had taken

place. Such messages might take many forms — a certain
wind blowing, for instance, or the call of a bird ...

Peter began to speak of other things. "Well, then the war
started and all them Watts went off to the war, all of them.
They gave me a house at Tobermary."

"How did you find working sheep after cattle?" I asked.

Peter snorted. "The bastards never stopped running
around. Stupid bloody things, sheep."

"What about drought?"

"Oh, there was a few, but they weren't that bad. 1929 was
the worst — we shifted 3,000 bloody cattle onto old Dynevor
Downs — not Dynevor where it is now. We shifted them to
that country right back on the other side of the lakes, and
we took a big mob of horses to agistment."

Peter told me about his first droving trip, to Quilpie in
1931. "When we got there we camped near the trucking
yards. This young bloke that was with us said to the cook:
'Where we going to put the bloody cattle?' So I said: 'In the
yards, aren't we?' He kept looking at the cattle wagons,
some with open doors, standing near the cattle yards. Those
wagons' floors were three foot off the ground." (This was
long before the days of road transport of cattle, and few if
any stations would have had loading ramps.) "Well, this
bloke, he said, 'How you gonna get the cattle in them
wagons?' — 'Well,' I said, 'you gotta lift the bastards up,
whaddya think?' " Peter gave a guffaw. "Of course, there
was a trucking race on the other side of the yards for the
cattle to walk up."

"After I was married we used to go to town in my car, a Ford

V8 utility I bought off the Watts for twenty quid. They practically gave it to me at that price. It had real good tyres and that, but no gas producer. They took it off before I bought it."

During World War II, there was a shortage of petrol and rationing was introduced. The gas producer was a metal tank about four feet by two feet broad and about one foot from front to back. It was mounted on the rear of the chassis, above the car's bumper bar.

"Did you know the car when it had the gas producer on it?" I asked Peter.

"My bloody oath didn't I! We had to get all them coals for it — first cut the timber, mulga stumps and all that, then dig a big hole, put in the wood, set it alight and cover it with dirt — and about four or five days later it was all bloody coals. Then we had to get it out of the hole and sift it — we used them old spring beds for that. We'd shovel the coals onto the beds and sift all the rubbish and ash out, then put the charcoal that was left into bags — that was what made the motor car run, by producing the gas.

"Well, after I bought the car I drove it into Quilpie and saw this old bloke. He had the garage there. He had one in Charleville, too. He said the engine was just about bug-gered. 'Why don't you put in a new engine?' he asked. — 'I haven't got the money,' I told him. He said: 'You'll be right. Pay me when you get the money.' It cost me ten quid for this new engine, and he put it all together for me. For years after, there was always people still coming along wanting to buy that car. Eventually I sold it to a bloke for 220 quid. Later still, when I'm in Charleville with Janie sick in the hospital, I'm walking home, see, and this bloke, he pulled up and gave me a lift. He said, 'What do you think of my car?' Well, I'm looking at the car as we're driving

Herb Wharton

Roy Mahar

Archie Dick

Ruby de Satge

Alf Barton

Peter Hood

Alice Gorringe

Peggy Gorringe

Wally Mailman

Jack Guttie

Branding fire, Ardmore Station, 1966. *(Photo: Roy Mahar)*

Roy Mahar (on horse), May Downs Station, 1968. *(Photo: Roy Mahar)*

Stock-camp horses, Ardmore Station, 1966. *(Photo: Roy Mahar)*

Ruby de Satge (centre) with her cousins Maud Dempsey and Patsy Craigie at Djarra. *(Courtesy R. de Satge)*

Left: Ruby de Satge at Djarra in 1938 or 1939. *(Courtesy R. de Satge)*

Stock-camp truck, Oben Station. Ruby de Satge is on the right. *(Courtesy R. de Satge)*

Georgina Fraser, Mabel Daley (camp cook) and stockmen bogged while moving camp, Oben Station. *(Courtesy R. de Satge)*

Above left: Peggy Gorringe, Alice Gorringe (nursing George), Bub and Mary Brown, 1949. *(Courtesy Peggy McKellar)*

Above right: Droving from Glengyle Station, early 1960s. Standing on left are George and Bill Gorringe. *(Courtesy Peggy McKellar)*

Wally Mailman riding a New Zealand bronco, with injured shoulder, 1960. *(Photo: Greg Russell)*

along. 'This is my bloody car!' I told him. 'How much you pay for it?' — '400 quid,' he said.

"Janie was in hospital a long time, and all the kids was in the hostel at Charleville. I had a job as barman at the Cattle Camp Hotel. Yeah, I was serving grog. They used to leave the keys to the kitchen cool room and the bar with me. On Christmas day they were away for a while and lots of Quilpie blokes came in, all wanting grog, but I told them we're not supposed to open. But then I said, 'Okay,' and they bought beer, rum, plonk — 180 quid's worth I sold that day. I told them blokes, 'Get out down the bloody river bank and do your drinking there.' It was only fifty yards away. Well, some of them was still in the bar when the boss walked in. 'Hey, what you doing opening up the bar? Policeman might come along.' Then I pulled all this cash out of my pocket. 'Hey, where'd this come from?' asked the boss. So I told him, and he gave me fifty quid out of it.

"I had to get money to pay boarding fees for the kids at the hostel. They'd come and stop with me at weekends — the publican never charged me for that. Janie was very sick for a long while. The Watts came along to see me a couple of times — they wanted me to go back to Tobermary, but I told them it was no good going back while my wife was sick in hospital. If I did go back and something happened to her, I'd have to turn round and return straight away. Even after she passed away they still wanted me back. At first I did think I'd go back to where I spent all those years, but then I thought maybe there were too many memories there. All my kids went to boarding school in Charleville except for my daughter Pat — she was taught Correspondence School lessons by old Mrs Watts — 'Mucha', as she was fondly known to the Aborigines. They was good times for me at Tobermary with the Watts, until my wife got sick. I

had money in them days, too, over 1000 quid in the bank.
I worked there for twenty-eight years."

"After that I went bush with my oldest daughter, Pat, and
worked around Quilpie for a while, and ended up as a
dogger on Mt Margaret Station. There were thousands of
sheep and cattle there. I was given a new Land Rover, wages,
and ten quid a head for trapping or shooting dingoes. I
needed money to keep the other kids at boarding school.
Another old dogger told me: 'All ya usually get in traps is
foxes, kangaroos and sheep', but within a week I trapped
my first dingo, only half a mile from the station homestead,
along the side of the road. For the rest of the short time I
was employed as a dogger, I caught ninety-six dingoes.
Some of 'em were real cunning, been fooling the other
doggers for years. I also got a lot of dingo pups. They was
also worth ten quid a scalp, so they was a real bonanza.

"One time, my daughter Dot was with me on holidays
and she was driving the Land Rover, following me across
country as I was tracking a dingo, gun in hand, noting
where it had chased and killed a sheep, had a feed, then
headed straight for the hillside. I got up to the hill and
noticed a small cave mouth. The tracks went up to it and I
heard the sound of dingo pups inside. It was too small for
me to crawl into — and I could see it went far back into the
hill. So I blocked up the cave mouth and set a trap to catch
the bitch. Next day I came back with a crowbar to widen the
cave mouth, then Dot wriggled in on her stomach until only
her ankles were left sticking out at the entrance. She
reached into the back of the cave and handed back to me
nine dingo pups, worth ninety quid. I had to pull Dot out
by the ankles. I didn't catch that bitch — she was a black

one and real cunning. Other doggers before me had tried plenty times to trap her."

"You really tried to catch that bitch?" I asked. I knew from experience that many old doggers were more cunning than the dogs they trapped. They could tell by the tracks and habits of the animal what sex it was, and some would sooner catch male dingoes than bitches — for if they trapped the bitch, no dingo pups next year, no bonuses and no job. Unlike domestic dogs, a dingo in the wild only mates and produces a litter once a year, usually in the winter months.

Peter didn't reply — he just laughed.

Peter recalled one of the great moments in his life, while working for the Peglers on Mumbla Station, in 1957.

"That's when we won the Quilpie Polo Gold Cup against all the cockies — they were never beaten for seven years before that, and afterwards they never played again."

"Who was in your team?" I asked. I knew that famous polo team had comprised mostly working men. In those days, polo was mainly played by station owners — there were big costs for transport and equipment. And as it was always a sport for the wealthy, there was no prize money, only trophies.

"There was me, Kenny Boggs, Jimmy Lowes and Tommy Donovan … can't remember the rest."

"Reminds me of that old poem 'The Geebung Polo Club'," I said, and recalled a few lines —

It was somewhere up the country
In the land of rock and scrub,
They formed an institution
Called the Geebung Polo Club.

Wild and wiry natives from
The rugged countryside —

"Yeh, yeh, it was a bit like that. Winning the Cup was a great moment for me. That night we took it along to the pub and Jimmy Coronies, the publican, filled it up three times with champagne."

"Which pub was it?" I asked. I remembered that the Coronies owned all three pubs in the town at one time. And I recalled an old tale, how Jimmy Coronies, on a trip to Brisbane, was asked: "Are you the Mr Coronies that belongs to Quilpie?" — "No," replied Mr Coronies, "you got it wrong, boy. Quilpie belongs to me."

"Well," Peter went on, "there we were in the pub, and most of the other cockies wouldn't drink with us, though some did fill up that Cup again with champagne. But we had no squatters in our team, see. And them cockies had trained polo horses, while we had just the bloody working man's work horses. A big mob of them new Australians was there then, and they filled the Cup four times more. They was fencing around the district — bloody hard workers, they was."

"After I been on Mumbla I went droving with Harry Thompson. He went to Yaraka and took delivery of 1,800 head of store cattle off the trains. We took them down the Cooper to Mt Howard, and then took a mob of fats from there to Quilpie.

"I done one trip as a train drover from Quilpie to Cunnamulla — it was an old steam engine. Well, I ended up with the engine driver and fireman in the cabin, with a bottle of rum. They got me shovelling coal into the fire. 'Ya gotta shovel with your left hand,' they told me, 'ya need your right hand for drinking.' " Peter laughed at the memory. "I was only a fireman until the bloody rum was finished.

"After that I went back to Quilpie and caught the DC3 to Leigh Creek, in South Australia. The others took about five weeks to walk seventy head of Harry's horses to Maree. They took me from Leigh Creek by car to Maree — they was nearly all Afghans living in Maree. We had to wait there for cattle coming in by train from Oodnadatta. Bloody terrible country at Maree — never see a tree, no creeks."

I nodded. On the Maree to Birdsville track there was no wood at times, and we only had cow-dung fires in the packhorse droving camp. This gave rise to the invention of the Bedourie oven, in preference to the heavy cast-iron camp oven, which was easily broken. The Bedourie oven proved light and durable, and only a small coal or cow-dung fire was needed for cooking.

On that trip, we were lucky. "One old Afghan at Maree owned the store and a truck, and he got us a load of wood for the camp eventually. We had 1,900 head of mixed cattle to take back to Nockatunga Station, and we went past Quinaby into New South Wales, past Mt Stuart and back into Queensland through the old customs house gate on the border fence. A boundary rider was there then, looking after the dingo barrier fence. The customs house was a big old ruined building, with bricks laying everywhere and apple trees round it. From there we went through the back of Bulloo Downs, and after about three months' droving we arrived at Nockatunga.

"After that I had my own droving plant for a while, and one time we took a mob of cattle to Cockburn, in South Australia. It was funny, that trip — we went down the South Australian side of the border fence, then crossed into New South Wales. Then, when we wanted to go back into South

Australia, near Cockburn, the stock inspectors seen the
negura burr on them cattle and we had to yard them on the
New South Wales side and pull out all them burrs — it took
days. Yet there was as much negura burr on the South
Australian side."

"Could have been clean negura burr," I suggested.

"Yeah — anyway, you didn't have to pull off the burr if
you went down the South Australian side of the border
fence."

"Another time I took a mob to Cockburn, half the cattle
was sent to Adelaide, and they asked me to bring the rest
back to Broken Hill and truck them there. That's where the
New South Wales line started, going to Sydney. There was
three different gauges for the South Australian, New South
Wales and Broken Hill lines. When we got to the trucking
yards at Broken Hill there was no engine to shunt them
wagons into place, so we gotta push them.

"Then I got a job train-droving from Broken Hill to
Orange. That's the frigging coldest place in Australia, that
bloody Orange. Lucky I had an old military greatcoat on.
Bloody freezing it was. I had to wait there for a train back
to Broken Hill. Still freezing, I walked into this Greek cafe
and the owner gave me a glass of rum and a big feed. I was
okay then."

"For a while I used to take three mobs a year from
Nockatunga. One year I took a mob of 1,100 cows past
Tibooburra, Broken Hill, Minindi way. Them cows were
bastards, and calving all the time. But I never lost any of
them, though I gave plenty of the calves away in exchange
for cakes and eggs from people along the way. I was getting
sick of eggs and I said to one of those farmers: 'Gee, youse

must have a big mob of fowls.' — 'Oh no, we're right down now, we only got about 6,000 left,' was the reply. I nearly fell off me horse.

"It was all right, droving in New South Wales. When I first started droving I had packhorses, but later I got a rubber-tyred wagon. One bad thing about New South Wales, though — sometimes you had to pay so much a head to water your stock. I drove a few mobs of fats into Quilpie and experienced a few cattle rushes … they was good old days."

As Peter went on telling me about those good old days, he described one special night horse who refused to walk between the sleeping herd and a wayward beast still feeding out in the dark. This reminded me of my own experience in my younger days. During my first droving trips, watching the cattle on cold, dark wintry nights, I would ride around on the night horse with the dull glow of the campfire beckoning from the camp, and above me the reflected light from a billion stars. The horse's head would be down in our slow death march around the sleeping herd. Then all of a sudden his head would come up and he'd veer off away from the herd and quicken his step. I couldn't see or hear anything in the darkness, and I'd try to steer him back on course, cursing his hard mouth. But good night horses had minds of their own — and soon I would discern the dark outline of a lone animal feeding away from the sleeping mob. No amount of urging could make that horse walk between that straying beast and the herd. That was one lesson I learned early, that a good night horse knew more about watching cattle at night than many of the men who rode him.

When transport began to play a large part in the droving life, Peter sold his droving plant and worked on Nockatunga Station — "Until," he told me, "one day the boss came along and found the head stockman drunk. I was out killing a bullock for meat when the boss drove up with that head stockman in his car. He said to me: 'You take over now. You're the head stockman.' Then he drove the few miles to the Noccundra pub and let the other chap off there, saying: 'Plenty of grog in there, go for your life.'

"The lease of that pub belonged to the owners of Nockatunga Station," Peter added, "and recently, when Kerry Packer bought Nockatunga, he also bought the pub. And talk of that pub reminds me of another thing. Nockatunga Station was then serviced by the Charleville flying doctor. But the Broken Hill flying doctor used to come in and land at the Noccundra pub. Well, there were quite a few people who thought it was much better to wait for the Broken Hill doctor than the one from Charleville!"

"Or maybe they thought the publican could fix 'em up better than any doctor," I suggested. "Tell me, how'd you like to be there now, giving Kerry Packer a gallop around on a polo horse?"

"Don't know. But I've heard he doesn't hafta ride his horses around from game to game — he flies them all over the place in an aeroplane." He paused. "Incidentally, one fellow who was one of the polo players that time we won the Gold Cup now works close by Nockatunga, on another station. He told me about something he and another stock-man encountered when they were mustering out there. Apparently that area is now overrun with oil workers and prospectors — seems that some aren't content with what benefits flow solely from wells in that oil- and gas-rich country.

"Well, this day, Kenny and his mate were mustering along a dry stony creek miles from anywhere when they came across what Kenny described as 'the Garden of Evil', miles from water in that desolate, drought-stricken arid region. They saw lush green foliage in sharp contrast to the drab, greyish mulga and gydgea leaves round about. It turned out to be a marijuana plantation, with a few wires strung around to keep cattle away. Every plant had a tin of water attached to a pole-drip, feeding it. The plantation was flourishing; whoever started it (and it could have been one of them oil workers) would only have to come round once a month to refill the water tins. Kenny told me that he and his mate wrecked the lot."

I might add that I have heard of other such gardens planted out in that so-called desert country, one even set up with a tractor and water pipes.

Peter's thoughts went back to his days as head stockman in the Nockatunga mustering camp. "We used to have six or seven Aboriginal stockmen from Doomadgee. We used a tractor to pull our 'bun cart', as we called the cook's wagon, from camp to camp. Bronco yards and bronco horses were still used for branding calves and cutting out on an open cattle camp. There'd be dust swirling, blokes galloping everywhere, lots of falls, sometimes broken bones and bruises, but nothing real serious. Some of them horses could buck all right when they were fresh, but after a day's work they were good horses to ride.

"Every three months we got our statements showing our wages and what we'd bought from the station store, tobacco and such. They'd ask, 'You want cheque?' I used to say, 'No bloody fear, can't cash a cheque in a mustering camp.' When them hawkers came around — that's when the money went. There'd be a big buy up, with everyone walking around in a brand-new pretty shirt, with red hankies around their necks." Peter laughed. "Proper ringers, all of them!

"There were good and bad seasons, you know. One year it was a real drought, we had to feed our horses while we mustered. Dingoes were everywhere, but we never worried about shooting them. They had to get a feed. They only killed the weak cattle that were going to die anyway. Like always, the rain did come, and when it did we were stuck around the station homestead for a month — we couldn't move for mud and water." Peter paused here, then added quietly: "That's the year we trucked away about 17,000 head of cattle. Droving was finished — it was all transport from then on." He sighed. "I was sorry to see the old droving days go, it was a good life and I really missed it."

"In the 1960s I went to Kihee Station. The boss owned some transport trucks so I ended up truck driving, taking cattle into the saleyards at Cunnamulla and Quilpie, but mostly to the meatworks at Bourke, in New South Wales. Bloody bastard of a road that was, all corrugated and dusty for a couple of hundred miles from Thargomindah. No bitumen roads then, only pot-holes and bulldust. At Hungerford they'd pull you up before you got to the border fence, and if you got there at night you'd probably have to wait till next morning for the policeman to inspect the brand and ear-marks. Bloody policeman there one time charged me two bob after inspecting the way bill."

"What for?" I asked.

"Buggered if I know." Peter shook his head. "But I remember some little kids who used to wait there and open the big dog-netting double gates for me. Their father worked on the dingo barrier fence and I used to throw them a few bob."

Neither of us could work out why the policeman had wanted that two-bob fee.

"I asked all them other truck drivers," Peter said, 'but none of them knew why."

"Maybe," I said, "that policeman thought them kids were onto a good racket and decided to do them out of a job. But seriously, what did you think of all that — taking cattle from Thargo to Bourke in one day, when it used to take a month in the droving days?"

Peter's answer was unequivocal. "Bloody terrible. Better in the old days when we walked the cattle in."

"After that," he went on, "I went to Durham Downs and worked for the Kidman mob again. The year before they'd sent a lot of cattle away on agistment to their other station. It was a good season: the Cooper had flooded, there was water and grass everywhere. We used to put the cattle out the back, at windmill watering places — all stones and spinifex and sandhills, that back country, and very few fences. But they always wanted to come back to the sweet country in the channels. We used packhorses in the Channel country, and trucks outside it. There was plenty of lignum growing in the channels and a lotta cleanskin bulls and cows in there, but the cunning bastards kept getting away. Real big floods come in that country, ya know — people are sometimes stranded for months. No mail, no all-weather road, no airstrip or helicopter."

I asked Peter about being stranded and what disasters resulted, but he only laughed and told me he never really felt stranded or isolated — there was always plenty of tucker while he sat around and waited for the floodwaters to go down.

"What do you think about today's helicopter and motor-bike mustering?" I asked him.

"No good," he replied. "Too much knocking about of the stock. It's so fast they try to keep the tail up with the lead, and no matter what, you can't do that. But they just let the bloody lead go to hell and west and crooked. And they still call themselves stockmen!"

After his experiences on Durham Downs, Peter worked on Bulloo Downs and a few places around Cunnamulla, then retired. Today, he lives with his grand-daughter, great-grandchildren and great-great grandchildren. A recent stroke he suffered has curtailed his activities, but his mind is as active as ever. He holds strong opinions on many issues, from land rights to education and law and order.

"Will land rights solve our problems, do you think?"

"Shit, no fear. You gotta have education first. Education in everything — blackfella history, whitefella history." He pointed into the distance in a vague westerly direction. "According to Murrie law I own all that country back there. But how we gonna get our own bloody stations established? We gotta have people with ability to look after them."

"One final question. Do you have any regrets about the past — would you change anything if you could go back?"

He gave his answer instantly. "If I lived my life over again I would not change a bloody thing. I never had much money, but I got lots of satisfaction from the jobs I done."

Peter Hood's contribution to the pastoral industry, and to Australia as a whole, has been outstanding. And he has achieved a great deal in helping to break down the stereo-typing of Aborigines in the outback. He succeeded in gaining his own rights — equal pay, equality and self-deter-mination — a lifetime ago.

Alice and Peggy Gorringe

―――――

The riches of King Someone's mines

It would take a whole book to do justice to the story of the Gorringe family — Alice and Peggy, their parents, brothers and sisters. It is a story of hardships, grief and fear, but also of love, happiness and achievement.

In this short account of the lives of Alice and Peggy, there is so much left unsaid. But Peggy has kept her diaries and letters over the years, and I am encouraging her to write the whole story herself. In the meantime, I have recorded this brief portrait.

All her life, Alice and Peggy's mother lived in dread, fearing that the government man would come to take away her children, her greatest treasures. During her own childhood in New South Wales she had seen this happen to a lot of her friends. " 'The government owns us, you know,' she used to say," Alice told me. "She and our Aunty Pearl were sometimes forced to sleep in the fork of a big tree, in case that government man came in the night to take them away."

I tried to imagine the feelings of those two little girls, Pearl and Ivy, not knowing when they might be taken from their old grandmother, with whom they lived while their mother worked for slave wages to help support the life-style of others.

"What a contrast to today!" Peggy remarked. "Today, our people have freedom to do what they want — go away on holidays, even just walk to a shop free of the knowledge that someone else is totally controlling their lives. Mum's fear was so deep inside her that she guarded her family all the time. I am proud to be one of her eleven kids."

Alice was only a toddler when Peggy, a January baby, was born in Cunnamulla in the 1930s, after her parents and their two small children had made a long and tiring journey from New South Wales. Originally, the family and their friends had lived in their own camps around the stations where the men were employed as stockmen. They had all been persuaded to go to a mission, where they were promised employment and housing. The group was rounded up from the stations and taken to the mission, but on arrival they found that they were expected to share accommodation and eat weevily food in a communal dining room. When the women asked for rations, wanting to prepare their own meals, the response was: "So you think you're better than everyone else!"

"That seems to be a failing of the whites," Peggy commented. "They expect different families to live together all the time. So then my parents and their friends planned to escape. They went about it very well. The men, working secretly with a sympathetic white man, got hold of an old truck that had been abandoned in the scrub. As they had no money, they scrounged spare parts and stored up petrol, while the women somehow managed to save flour, tea and a few tins of meat. All this took a long time.

"At last they were ready. One night they sneaked away

from the mission, heading for the Queensland border and what they hoped would be freedom."

I imagined that old T-model Ford, minus its windscreen and hood, with running boards and a flat tray top, chugging along only at night with no lights on the car. One of the group would be standing on the running board with a torch, lighting the way to freedom.

"During the day they hid near stations or outside small towns. They had no money but lots of hope. The men would sneak into the homestead or town to steal petrol and rations."

And that was how they arrived at Cunnamulla.

The group found a degree of freedom in Queensland, yet the government had the power to send them back to the mission, and that threat always hung over them.

It was just before their sister Bubsy was born that Alice and Peggy's parents went their separate ways. Ivy, their mother, lived with the children in Tibooburra. Bubsy, suffering from malnutrition, had to go to hospital at Broken Hill, and was there a long time. Peggy remembers their poverty and hunger as their mother worked hard at house-cleaning and washing to provide for them all.

It was at Broken Hill that they met Bill, the man who was to have such an influence in helping to shape their lives. To us, he was the most admired stockman in western Queensland. A little later they all went to live with him at Arrabury Station, in the Channel country of south-west Queensland.

Here Alice took up the story. "One day Mum and us kids climbed onto the back of the mail truck in Tibooburra, along with two stockmen heading out to work. We were sitting amid petrol drums, boxes of station rations, bags of potatoes and onions, mail-bags, swags, spare parts — you name it. To begin with we were trying unsuccessfully to escape the swirling red dust of that dirt road as the truck went charging through the changing landscape. It was a long journey, it took over a week. Through Naryilco, over the Cooper Creek to Nappa Merrie, then on … But on the way it rained, well, the dust turned to mud and we got stranded on a sandhill miles from anywhere, forced to camp for a few days until the road dried out."

Alice remembered those few days well. "There was plenty of potatoes, onions and flour on board, but we didn't have much in the way of cooking gear. The men cut open a four-gallon kerosene tin, burnt it and washed it out. To add some meat to the vegies they managed to catch one single rabbit — they didn't have a rifle — and into the kerosene tin that rabbit went, along with the vegies to make a stew. Well, that lasted the four adults and five children two or three days. Luckily there was plenty of flour on the truck, and Mum made lots of johnnie cakes, cooked on the coals. There was plenty of tea, too."

Finally they arrived at Arrabury Station and joined up with the man they learned to call "Dad".

Peggy spoke of Dad with great affection. "He had a son, Harry, who was much older than us," Peggy told me. "He treated us just as though we were his own brothers and sisters, spoiling us all in different ways. "There were five kids in Mum's family, including me and Alice, and over the years we had four more brothers and two sisters. We were all treated with the same loving care, and we all received the same discipline from Mum and Dad."

Alice smiled. "Mum would even flog us all at the same

time whenever any one of us played up. She probably reckoned it would save time!"

"We learned to look out for each other as we grew up, and we are still close," Peggy added. "All the times I've needed strength, I have had eleven strong loved ones to turn to."

Both Alice and Peggy have vivid memories of life at Arrabury. For the first time they had more than enough food. Food seemed to be everywhere, outside as well as in the house. They were taken hunting for bush tucker by an old Aboriginal couple, who told them that becuase they were girls, they must not go near a certain big, beautiful tree. The reasons remained unexplained. They were told not even to look up at it.

"Shortly before we came to Arrabury," Peggy told me, "a woman had broken the taboo and gone to sit under the tree — and a little while later, for no apparent medical reason, she died. The doctor called this a mysterious death, but it was no mystery to the old people in the area." Years later, when they were out riding, the same old man would call out, coaxing them to go around that same tree instead of riding past it.

"After that old man died," Alice told me, "we would still see him at the chook yard and at the cattle yards — during the day and at night he used to appear to us. Musta been watching over us!"

At Arrabury, horses and cattle became an everyday part of the two girls' lives. Neither of them could say exactly when they first began to ride — but Alice certainly recalls her first real buster.

She and her brother John were driving some horses along one day — Alice was on an old retired racehorse called Daisy, very hard-mouthed. All the horses suddenly began to canter, with John riding up behind them. Then Daisy took off flat-out, bolting after the others and passing them. As Alice, yelling in terror, flashed past, Johnny called out: "Don't worry, Sis, she'll pull up at the gate!"

"Well," Alice told me, "she bolted past all them horses and headed down the track to the gate. And she did pull up. But not as I'd have liked her to. She raced flat-out right up to the gate, and I thought she'd crash through it, but at the last minute she swerved and skidded to a halt, while I kept going straight ahead. My first real buster — and luckily no injury."

Peggy laughed. "Falling off horses became a part of learning to ride them, but no serious damage was ever done, though Alice said I was once knocked out by a brumby mare that bucked and threw me. All I remember of it was when I came to and looked down the road, still dazed and blurry-eyed, I could see something bobbing up and down and coming closer and closer … and at last I realised it was Mum, her plump figure running towards me with a billy can of water in each hand, wearing her old floppy hat and with a frantic look on her face. It's a scene I still recall and laugh about. Yes, it seemed comical, but I realise now that Mum must have had a terrible life, worrying about us kids all the time."

Over the years, the Gorringe family spent their time even as kids breaking in horses for their Dad; he owned a mob of horses which were added to from time to time by running down young brumbies from the herds and acquiring new animals that way. And not only did the two girls have to learn about horses and cattle, they had to become bush mechanics as well.

Alice described her and her brother John's first lesson in mechanics. When they were about eight and ten years old respectively, they were taught to drive the old station Land Rover, their feet barely able to reach the clutch to change gears. Sometimes one of them would press down the clutch while the other manipulated the gear lever. They were always being roused on for riding the clutch as they took off. "You'll break the bloody axle!" Bill would yell. One day, four miles from home, the axle did break and they had to walk home.

Next day, they were taken back to the broken-down Land Rover in the station truck. "Here's a spare axle," Bill told them. "You jack up the chassis, undo the nuts and bolts, then pull out the old axle, and put this one in. You'll need these spanners." Then he walked away to a shady tree, boiled the billy and rested until they had completed the task.

"Funny thing," said Alice, "I don't think either of us broke an axle again. But that was how we learned to do lots of things. We might have a broken bridle rein, say — we'd run to the old man, but he wouldn't fix it for us. Instead, he'd show us how to mend it ourselves. He even taught us to make greenhide rope and how to canterline saddles. Yet life didn't seem too hard as we grew up. In fact, we can look back and say we were lucky to have a Mum and Dad to teach us the values of life. They were high on principles, you know. They taught us the value of a quid — but they also taught us that family and friendships are more important than money." She smiled. Maybe Mum and Dad didn't always practise what they preached, but we turned out okay.

Peggy took up the story. "We've lost them both now, of course. Our Dad was a big, quiet man. Somehow he could make me confess to whatever sin I'd committed just by giving me a stern look. I'd say he was the smartest man in Western Queensland. There are heaps of stories told about his feats in the bush. How he once rode an outlaw horse outside the Birdsville pub, for instance … At eighty-two he was still horse-breaking and driving around. His driving! Well, that's another story. Everyone knew about that."

I myself recall being in Windorah one day when an old-time stockman warned me: "Don't you ever hitch a ride with that old bloke Bill if you want to get anywhere in a hurry — he pulls up all the time for nothing. He's always going off the road to boil the billy."

So when Peggy related the following story I could quite believe it.

"Traffic indicators were things Dad could well do without as he drove around town at a snail's pace," she told me. "He didn't really need a speedometer either — out on the open road his top speed was about forty kilometres an hour, and he used to tell how fast he was going by the wind force as he held his right arm out of the car window. As for going on journeys with him during the cricket season — that was a series of real horror trips for us impatient kids. We learned to make excuses not to go along with him if there was a test match on. Just before 10 o'clock, no matter where we were, Dad would drive off the road, pull up under a shady tree, and there he'd stay until the end of the day's play, listening to his old valve radio with the aerial slung over a tree branch. We kids would have to amuse ourselves as best we could — we were always hoping rain would stop play in whatever city the cricket was being played."

Alice nodded as Peggy went on: "I can still see him in memory, laying on his swag, one leg crossed over his other bent knee, his hat covering his face and that old radio crackling out static and the cricket commentary. I'm sure he dozed most of the day, only getting up for a sandwich. When the sun began to dip low in the sky he'd rise and tell us how much he had enjoyed the cricket. There'd be shouts of glee from us kids when the stumps were drawn and we'd be on our way at last." Peggy smiled. "It's strange, you know, in them days us kids all cursed the test matches, but today I'm a cricket fan myself."

"Our mother taught us a lot as well," Alice said. "Short and plump she was, and she always had this floppy-brimmed rag hat on her head. She was teacher, nurse, horse saddler, even riding instructor, though she never rode a horse in her life. After we moved to Windorah, we all used to go on droving trips, travelling around in a horse-drawn wagon. First off, the cattle would be drafted out on the flat in order to get the mob together so that we could drove them to their destination. There'd be horses cattle and kids everywhere, dust rising and some of us getting plenty of busters. And there Mum would be, standing near the camp directing the traffic, waving a tea-towel or her old rag hat, trying to attract someone's attention. She'd yell instructions at the top of her voice — "WATCH OUT FOR THE FENCE! LOOK OUT FOR THAT LOW TELEPHONE WIRE DANGLING DOWN! MIND THE GULLIES! WATCH THEM TREES!"

"Finally, Dad would get annoyed. 'Stop that!' he'd call, and he'd ride over to Mum. Then, while the rest of us went on with the drafting, they'd have a row, which always ended with Mum accusing Dad of trying to kill her kids.

"Of course we enjoyed every minute of drafting, galloping about and chasing cattle all over the place. In fact, we sometimes let a bullock get away so that we could bring him back flat-out, regardless of broken ground, fences, low-lying telephone lines or trees. We loved the chase. But it didn't matter that some of us were now in our teens — we were still Mum's babies, her greatest treasures. And I think her fear of Dad getting us killed on horseback was almost as great as her dread that the government man would come to take us away."

As Peggy remarked, being part of such a large and diverse family had both advantages and disadvantages. "When we were in the bush we looked out for each other, depending on one another. When we moved to Windorah and went to school, the one big plus was that you could afford to fight with your brothers and sisters and still there'd be other children to play with.

"We had a childhood like that of most bush children," Alice said. "Short on schooling and long on working, from sunrise to sunset every day of the year. There was no television and few books. Books were used to light the fire if we didn't move or work when we were asked to do so. If we had a book, we'd hide it. We used to like meeting other drovers, to get books we never seen.

"Like most station children, we made toys out of mud, wood, tins, string and wire. We had goats, poddy calves, unlimited horses and cattle around us as we played. And there were few fences: our backyard stretched across the channel country of far south-west Queensland."

Peggy fondly recalls Harry, Bill's son and the oldest of that big family group. She remembers his return home after serving in World War II. "He was a huge, gentle man. He had a donkey team that he used for grading bush tracks, dragging a triangular-shaped piece of iron. They also pulled a big old wagon carrying fencing posts. Sometimes Harry would take the kids out with him — and Peggy remembers how, when they were with him, they could indulge in the luxury of eating as much tinned fruit and condensed milk as they liked. Afterwards, Harry started his own droving plant, then married and had a family of his own. Later still he worked on the railway at Quilpie.

Whenever school holidays came round they would all go bush, with their mother driving four horses that pulled the wagon. Both Alice and Peggy recalled one memorable trip across the trackless Coopers Creek channels in that rubber-tyred wagon.

"We were going from Morney to Quilpie with a mob of cattle. Most drovers used pack horses to cross the channel country — creek after creek, black cracky ground, lignum and coolabah trees. Well, we got so many punctures that we ran out of patches. We started putting grass in the tyres, but that wasn't any good, didn't last long — so eventually all us kids on horseback had to give up our saddle blankets to stuff in the tyres, binding them up with wire. And that was how we got across them channels."

"But there was a big drawback to using our saddle blankets," Alice said. "When we finished droving for that year we had to canterline all them saddles. But cross them channels we did. Every time we came to a creek, Mum would offload the little kids, drive down to the creek bed and then sometimes she'd have to travel quite a way before she could get up on the opposite bank. But like the bushwoman she was, she got where she wanted to go."

The part of Coopers Creek where this happened is about thirty miles across. Most drovers used pack horses here, as Peggy said — there was no road, and no crossings. Some people are known to have become lost attempting to negotiate these channels.

That was only one of many holiday droving trips for the Gorringe kids. By now, Bill was droving full-time, mostly for the Kidman mob. Alice was the horse-tailer on most of these

trips. Unlike Peggy, she did not go to school in Windorah.
Her schoolroom was the stock-route.

Peggy recalled other incidents from the times she went
droving as a kid. Like the time one of her brothers brought
his New Australian friend, Karl, out from Quilpie for the
school holidays. "Karl soon learned to sit a horse well
enough to ride around them big, fat, quiet bullocks," she
told me. "So one night after the cattle had settled down to
camp, Dad told him: 'Your turn now, Karl. You go and do
this watch.' Then, seeing that the boy didn't understand
what doing a watch meant, Dad explained and handed him
his treasured timepiece in its leather case, a pocket watch
that he always wore on his belt.

"Karl mounted the night horse, then asked: 'What am I
supposed to do?' He really didn't understand droving all
that well, you know. — 'Oh, ya gotta do the watch, riding
around the cattle,' Dad told him, then settled down at the
campfire, knowing that the experienced night horse would
take care of the kid. Well, that kid rode around the herd
once, then he pulled up at the campfire and asked for a
pocket knife. Off he rode again to the sleeping herd, and
stayed away for about half an hour. Then he rode back to
the campfire, where the rest of us were eating and talking.
'I have finished doing the watch,' he announced proudly,
and handed back to Dad his precious timepiece, which he
had levered apart with the pocket knife.

"Well, you should have heard the uproar from Dad!
Luckily he had another pocket watch. But that was one
cattle watch I'll always remember," Peggy told me, laughing.

"We had some near-tragedies too," Alice told me. "We can laugh at them now, but they weren't funny at the time." On one trip we went on, Mum had driven across the trackless channels in that same old horse-drawn wagon, and we'd camped near Eromanga. Well, in the morning the cattle were moving off camp and Mum was in the wagon with the three or four smallest kids. She was all packed up, with the horses harnessed and ready to go when one of them began to jib, prancing up and down on the same spot. Mum was sitting on the wooden seat in front and all the kids were in the back amid the swags and rations. Mum was talking to the horses, trying to coax them to move off, when my brother John, standing nearby with a stockwhip, gave that prancing horse a couple of quick cracks up the ribs. Well, away them old carthorses went, bolting flat-out — and there was Mum sitting back on the reins, trying to control them."

Alice recalled that she had been with the cattle on the opposite side of the fence. She sat on her horse thinking: "Oh gawd, she's gonna run into a gydgea tree or the fence and capsize and the whole lot of them will be killed!"

"Mum was calling out: 'Whoa, whoa, whoa!' and straining on the reins, with her foot pressed down hard on the brake lever, and all them little kids were standing up, hanging onto the driver's seat and yelling: 'Gib it to 'em, Mum, gib it to 'em!' and enjoying every minute of their wild ride. 'Course, they'd no idea of the danger they was in. Finally, Mum managed to swing them bolting horses onto a graded track. John had mounted up and taken off after the wagon, and with Mum still calling out 'Whoa, whoa!' and the kids shrieking and laughing, he brought the bolting horses to a halt. As Mum sat there sighing with relief, John said: 'Just like in them cowboy movies, hey Mum?'"

Both Alice and Peggy recall getting their first riding

boots, at Planet Downs. They were size five, and both of them were eager to let me know that they still wore size five boots. I didn't find this difficult to believe, and I related my own story of my first pair of riding boots. I had scavenged them — a pair, well worn they was, with the toes turned up and the heels turned over. Size seven ... and when I rode my last horse I was still wearing the same size.

But those new boots the girls were given mostly hung from the sides of their saddles as they rode barefoot — they remember the lignum tearing at their toes as they rode around the Channel country. Whenever they approached a station homestead or a car drew near, or they saw other stockmen and drovers coming, Bill would rouse: "Put ya boots on, put ya boots on, somebody's coming — station up ahead!" He thought you weren't properly dressed without riding boots on your feet.

"But to us kids them riding boots seemed better dangling from our saddles," Peggy said. And she nodded: "Dad used to fashion sandals for us, too, out of thick harness leather and we'd add a few straps."

An unforgettable experience occurred when the two girls were out mustering with Bill and another much older Aboriginal stockman. The vast cattle empire they rode through was once his ancestral tribal kingdom. This day Alice, Peggy, Bill and the old stockman pulled up at a rocky hill. The old Aborigine said to the two girls: "Go into that hill and have a look at what's inside."

Peggy takes up the story. "Well, we didn't see how we could get inside the hill, but then he showed us a small cave with a hidden entrance."

"The sort of place a dingo bitch would nose out to have her pups," Alice put in.

That old stockman told us what we would find inside the cave after we managed to get past its mouth, which was too small for anyone to get through except a child. We were filled with excitement, and crawled through the mouth of the cave on our bellies. Six or seven feet into the hill, just where the cave opened out, there was this jagged pointed rock hanging from the ceiling like a spear. We had been warned about it by the old stockman, and knew we must avoid touching it at all costs. We had to crawl beneath it. If our bodies had come in contact with the guardian rock, our backs would be broken and we would be paralysed and die."

So they crawled under the rock and found themselves in what they coud only describe as an ancient conference room, with what appeared to be man-made ledges for seating cut into the rock all around the cave wall. They stared in astonishment through the stifling dust that was stirred up when they moved. A dim, eerie light came from a small vent above, in the top of the hill, and they saw another larger passage leading off to the left, just as the old man had described, to a bigger cave — and beyond that, he had told them, was a third cave in which lay the treasure of that ancient Aboriginal kingdom.

It was strange and frightening, standing beneath that air vent. Then the two men waiting on the hill-top above dislodged a shower of pebbles, which came down the air vent. This stirred up more dust and the girls, coughing, gasping and afraid, crawled back to the entrance, once again avoiding contact with the guardian rock, then scrambled outside to gulp in fresh air.

"Well, what did you see?" the old man asked them. "It

was just as you described it," they replied, "so far as we went."

This, of course, raises the question: how did the old stockman know about the cave, unless he had been told about it by some equally ancient tribesman when he was a child? And how were those ledges made around the cave, and how did the supposed treasure get there? Perhaps there was another concealed entrance to the cave. It seems improbable that only kids or pygmies made and used that antique conference room in the Australian inland.

I find the story of that cave as incredible as any tale of lost treasure in the history of mankind. For years I had heard stories about that cave and other hidden places and what they might contain. One old Aborigine once told me: "I know what lies inside that inner cave." But he did not tell me or anyone else. And neither Alice nor Peggy have ever felt an urge to seek out those supposed riches, for both declare whatever treasure may lie there, it is not their's to touch.

Over the years I have pondered on the mystery. Why would Aborigines have amassed riches in a society where they were meaningless and could not be used to acquire anything? Did the treasure consist of gold, opal and other stones, ochres, rock carvings and paintings?

One story, fact or fiction, states that after the invasion by the English, treasures were hidden across the land, often transported thousands of miles, taken to other caves, tossed into now dried-up waterholes or buried under unusual clumps of trees, away from the greedy eyes of the advancing white men. Some point out landmarks showing the path of this remarkable transportation across vast distances. (I myself have certainly seen some unusual landmarks across the outback.) If all this were true, it would make other tales of other lost treasure pale by comparison. And who am I to doubt the words and wisdom of my ancestors, who survived and flourished since the Dreamtime, long, long before the coming of the white races?

One tale relating to this story of hidden treasure tells how a lump of gold half the size of a horse's head once stood on a ledge above a waterhole, a permanent Aboriginal camping place. The kids used to play with it. Then, according to oral history, as the white explorers advanced towards the interior, the huge nugget was pushed off the ledge into the waterhole. After the explorers came other white people with sheep and cattle. The country was over-grazed and the waterhole dried up. Today, it is only a depression in the ground. Is it possible a gigantic gold nugget lies beneath the silt erosion of man-made drought?

I suppose that some Aboriginal prophet or philosopher of ancient times might somehow have known about the outside world and the value of gold and gems, perhaps through contact with mariners long before Cook landed on Australian shores. It would not have been so difficult for such an Aborigine to amass gold and gems — after all, if a few inexperienced gold diggers around the 1850s were able to make their foruntes in a very short time, how much easier it would have been for the people who had lived on the continent since the dreamtime to do the same. We should not forget that Aborigines solved the riddle of aero-dynamics with the comeback boomerang, thousands of years before the invention of the stone wheel and long before the first aeroplane was designed.

But if all this were true, what would be the purpose of amassing the treasure? Perhaps, somewhere in the inland, a new Aboriginal kingdom was to be founded, with a new way of life based on monetary values. The sites of these buried treasures stretch in a straight line for thousands of kilometres across the sparsely populated inland, from southern Victoria across outback New South Wales and Queensland. Could this have been the route of a prophet heading for the red heart of Uluru — or possibly that of some lost mariner attempting, with the help of the Aborigines, to transport his newly discovered riches home to Asia? Perhaps this speculation is not too far-fetched when you recall the tales of white convicts and criminals who escaped from custody, setting out in their ignorance to walk to China.

Who can say how much of these tales of treasure is truth, how much is myth? I have certainly seen some unusual landmarks across the outback. And thousands of years ago it would have been easy for someone, with Aboriginal help, to amass vast riches merely by scratching the surface of the earth. I have been fortunate to have seen so much of the outback country on horseback. I have often seen traces of opal and minerals of all kinds, but I was never tempted to start digging there and then — though there were many times when I said to myself, "One day I'll come back to this spot and maybe dig a hole in the ground."

Consider, too, that the Aborigines did in fact mine many things, including thousands of stone axe heads from one particular area in northwest Queensland. Over thousands of years of walking over the land, they would collectively have known about or seen practically every rock on the surface of their tribal territories. (And through the ages, drought, flood and bushfire would have covered or revealed what lay beneath the ground.) So maybe these tales are not so fanciful. But in any case, I share the viewpoint of Alice and Peggy, that if such treasures do exist, secreted from prying eyes, they are not their's nor mine to touch.

This was not the only adventure Alice and Peggy recalled around that sacred place. One time, while droving horses from one station to another, the station horses were yarded and the quiet drovers' horses hobbled out each night. This particular morning, there was grass and water everywhere and the quiet horses, hobbled, were feeding close by. As there was no hurry, they decided to let the station horses feed around the camp as well, while they had breakfast. So the two mobs of horses fed contentedly within sight of the sacred cave. Suddenly a screeching flock of black cockatoos came from the south. They were flying so low that both the horses and the people around the campfire became alarmed. Then the station horses took off, galloping, and the plant horses followed them. It took an eight-mile walk to catch up with the quiet horses, and another day to round up the station horses. It seemed as if those black cockatoos had flown over just to startle the horses — and they had succeeded. The two girls did not think it strange that this should happen within sight of that awesome cave.

"Perhaps it was a message, a sign of powers beyond our control," Alice said.

Out riding with her brother John one day, Alice recalled how they came across an incredible sight on the slopes of a stony hill on Planet Downs. It was late winter and the hillside seemed to be crawling with dingo pups — "worth a quid a head," as Alice remarked. Although they never had any money and had no real need of it out in the bush, they both realised that here was a small fortune running wild on that stony hillside. So after those dingo pups they raced, up and down the slopes with stirrup irons pulled from their saddles and swinging on the ends of the leathers. They soon had plenty of scalps.

At last, with the horses tired and lamed from rushing over the rocky ground, they gathered up the scalps and headed slowly home, planning what they would do with their newly acquired fortune. Alas, when they got home, Dad was not at all impressed by their haul of dingo scalps, but he was very concerned about the knocked-up, shin-sore horses, and both Alice and John got a hiding instead of the praise they'd expected.

Wild dingoes have only one litter of pups a year, usually towards the end of winter. Dingo trappers were employed — sometimes they used traps, sometimes poison. In the 1960s, millions of poison baits were dropped from aircraft in the outback Channel country of Queensland. It was said that goannas and crows thrived on them — until the introduction of the lethal poison 10–80. In the 1920s, when cattle were sold for around five quid a head, the bounty for dingo scalps was one or two quid each, and this stayed much the same until a few years ago. By then the price of a bullock had risen to $600, so station stockmen had no incentive to help control the dingo, something which could easily have been achieved if the bounty had been raised. But the high-ups were against offering too much money to the working men and women. Yet compare the simple solution of raising the bounty against the cost of aerial dropping of baits, and the possible long-term effects of so much poison on the earth.

One thing I have noticed out in that country is that when the dingo ruled, there would be a few kangaroos and emus, and fewer feral pigs, foxes, goats or cats. Today, much of the bird life of that same country is threatened by the feral cat. Now, if a birdwatcher shines a torch up into the branches of a tree, hoping to observe a night bird, all he or she will see are the glowing eyes of maybe thirty or forty feral cats. Will they now offer a bounty for cats, or will they drop more poison baits?

In 1953, Alice, Peggy and Bill set off with the packhorses for Yaraka, at the end of the railway line in central Western Queensland. There they took delivery of 300 bulls and walked them to Naryilco Station, in the furthest corner of south-west Queensland, where the borders of South Australia, New South Wales and Queensland meet. (As someone once remarked, the state borders always meet there, but very few people do. This is true even today.)

As the crow flies, that trip would be about 600 kilometres, but it was much further the way they travelled, following the channels of Cooper Creek most of the way, with no roads to follow amidst the wide expanse of flooded country. Bill seemed to know where every old wire-and-stub post yard was situated in that maze of channels. Many had been disused for years. They saw hardly anyone as they headed downstream, with water and grass everywhere.

"The bulls were quiet and it was a great droving trip," Peggy recalled.

Yet one incident occurred which Alice and Peggy still laugh about today. This took place soon after they began following the Barcoo River down. They passed a boundary rider's hut and he came out to talk to them and to see them through the station. He had a nephew from Brisbane staying with him, and he said that for a whole week he had been trying to get the youth out and about. Now he suggested the nephew might come with him to see the drovers through the station. But the lad declined, sure that there would be nothing in a drover's camp to interest him. He said he'd seen it all before: nothing but dogs, swags, cattle, horses and stockmen. But somehow he was persuaded, and a little while later he rode out with his uncle. Alice and Peggy both recall that first encounter with the young city slicker.

"When he got to our camp and seen us girls, he was flabbergasted!" All he could say in a breathless voice was 'Girls! Oh, girls!' Well, we couldn't keep him away from the camp after that. For days on end he'd catch us up and ride with us, then he'd go home at sundown. Next day he'd be there again — he was a real pain in the arse. Finally we swam the cattle over a waterhole to get off the stockroute; this way we thought we'd lose him. But no — a few hours later, there he was. He'd tracked the cattle and swum across to join us. It got that way, we couldn't have a swim or use the toilet, we didn't know when or where he'd turn up. But at last we left him behind and reached Windorah, where Johnnie and Archie Guttie joined us. Then we went on to Naryilco and from there we took a mob of fat cattle to the trucking yards at Bourke, in New South Wales."

While they were waiting at Naryilco for that mob of cattle, Alice recalled that they started breaking in some fresh horses. "One day Peggy was riding this colt — he was outside the yard for the first time. Well, he took off, pig-rooting and bolting around the ridges and over the hills, until he was out of sight. Me and John became worried and wanted to go after Peggy, but Dad said: 'It's no good you galloping after her, that horse would see or hear you coming and only gallop faster. She'll be right, the horse will pull up at a fence.' However, the nearest fence in that direction was ten miles away, and in the other direction fifty miles. Me and John were really worried. That colt had no mouth, he was only roughly broken. In them days we'd just run them in the yard, rope them, then bag them down, mouth them overnight and get them working.

"We were very relieved when Peggy returned about four hours later, on a much more docile horse. She told us how she'd been unable to turn the colt after it galloped away, so when she wanted to make him go in a particular direction, she hit on the idea of taking off her hat and placing it over one of his eyes. The horse would then veer off, and that was how she steered him home."

In the space of a few months they had had to outdistance a lovelorn city slicker and Peg had had to steer a bolting, bucking horse with the aid of her hat. And then, in Bourke for the first time, they experienced at first-hand the ugly face of racism. After trucking the cattle, they walked into the first cafe they came to, pockets full of money, wanting ice-creams and milkshakes. Only to be told: "You'll have to go down the street, we don't serve blacks in here." Two doors down they found another cafe where they enjoyed their feast among their own lot. They also discovered that at the picture show the audience was segregated, black and white. It was unlike their own country, where there was no such blatant racism as they were growing up.

Later that same year they drove a mob of fats from Durham Downs to Cockburn, in South Australia. That was the coldest trip the girls ever experienced. In the end, to avoid the biting south wind they were mostly heading into, they wore their coats and jumpers back to front to keep out the chill.

A few years after more trips from Naryilco to Bourke again, and from Morney to Naryilco, they spent one Christmas in Tibooburra. They recalled little relations from around the town watching and helping them as they hobbled and unhobbled the horses. "What you fellas putting bangles on their legs for?" one kid asked.

Peggy told me: "Not long after that we camped for a while at Milparinka, for the annual bush races. Dad owned one horse he thought was fast — it was called Said Ali, after an Indian hawker who used to travel that corner of New South Wales up into Queensland. He had a camel-drawn wagon and sold his wares at outback towns, stations and mustering and droving camps. I remember that over the years he had several dogs, but every one was named Tiger. Well, Said Ali didn't win a single race at Milparinka." She smiled as she added: "Life was never dull for us as we grew up on the stockroutes, you know. Once we were even lucky enough to be passing through Thargomindah when there was a dance on, so that was one night when we wore dresses and shoes!"

One horrific night Peggy will always remember. It was when they were droving a mob of what she and many others claim to be the worst cattle in the west, from Waverney. "At first them cattle weren't too bad, but one night we camped on Springvale — you know, there's a windmill there, not far from the main highway, near the Jump-up."

I nodded. "Yeah, there's a native well there in the middle of the road."

"That's the place. And sometimes you can see the Min-Min light there. Well, I was watching the cattle this night, and they suddenly took off, rushing straight towards me — it was all mulga and timber close by. As I tried to get out of their path the horse I was on fell. I thought of those cowboy movies, with cattle stampeding through everything in their way, and I began to think, 'This is it. The end.' But you know, everything happened too quick for me to feel really frightened.

"The nighthorse managed to regain his feet and stood for a while, and I grabbed the bridle reins and remounted. By then the herd had passed on either side of us — all you could hear was the cracking of the mulga branches and the thunder of galloping hooves.

"I was really shaken. Dad, riding a second night horse, came galloping up. 'Are you all right, girl?' — 'Yes, yes,' " I said, finding my voice. — 'Well,' he went on as he galloped past, 'you should be up trying to turn the lead, not moping around on the tail here.' So we took off after the cattle, which by now had split into two or three mobs. We spent the rest of the night and half the next day gathering them up.

"After that, handling that mob of cattle by day or night became a nightmare for all of us. Them cattle would rush for no apparent reason. We had to double and triple the watch at night, but still they'd rush. To make matters worse, we were now into the smaller, more settled station areas, with fences everywhere. Day and night them cattle knocked down fences and we had to repair them. It go so bad we would sometimes fall asleep riding along on horseback during the daytime. Then, the final night before we trucked them cattle in Quilpie, we camped at Orange Tank. That was one of the worst of all the rushes we'd had — some of the cattle were trampled to death and others were crippled. It was like Christmas had arrived when we yarded those cattle behind the big, strong steel yards next day and trucked them away."

Peggy talked about the summer months. "When droving was finished for the year we were mostly busy mustering and breaking in our horses and branding the young ones. For weeks at a time we'd camp down in the unfenced channels, keeping out the brumby stallions who would try to entice our mares away. We'd swim and fish in the waterholes — I can tell you we preferred all that to being at home in town, doing housework!

"Sometimes Dad took on fencing jobs, cutting posts and we'd help him, cutting posts. And on top of all this we'd have to repair saddles and bridles and so forth. — That was our summer holidays, you might say."

It was while the girls were out cutting posts one day that they came across a team of New Australians, who were also busy fencing in the same area. They recall that meeting in the middle of nowhere very well. The two girls were busy wielding their axes as the New Australians drove up in their truck and got out, yabbering away in their own lingo. They came towards the girls, still talking loudly and with their hands outstretched.

"No, no, ya not getting my bloody axe!" Alice and Peggy both shouted, thinking the men were trying to take away those axes they'd been swinging all day.

The blokes kept yabbering away, pleading for the axes, with the girls telling them to get their own bloody axes, until finally Bill intervened. "It's okay," he said, "they only want to cut some posts for you — they're not used to seeing women do this work. They don't want to keep your axes."

Alice grinned. "It was a bit of a shock to us, meeting gentlemen ... though I have to say that most of the blokes we met over the years were decent, respectable men."

So they continued their droving life, travelling up north to Winton, down south to Bourke, Broken Hill and Cockburn. There were good trips and bad. The worst were those Waveney cattle, the best that mob of quiet bulls.

Peggy talked about the good and bad cooks they had to

appreciate or endure in the mustering and droving camps when their mother stayed at home and the younger kids were at school.

One remarkable cook was Archie Guttie. "No matter how dusty or dry the weather, Archie would always be wearing a clean white apron. At meal times he'd rest on his shovel handle, watching that everyone, including the bosses, cut their meat and bread properly. He was a great cook. I remember on one packhorse droving trip, he carried the short-handled broom stuck in his pack saddle, and each camp we came to he would sweep the ground around the fire and table. Sometimes as we rode into camp our spurs would be trailing in the dust, and he'd make us take them off or turn them around so they didn't stir up the dust around the fire and the food."

As horse-tailer, Alice was always the last to appear for breakfast. Sometimes the cattle would be on their way and the cook only waiting for her to eat before he could start off as well. She told how one particular morning, feeling cranky, she told the cook: "I'm not eating this bloody half-cold steak that's sitting on the grill iron." — "Okay," he said. He promptly threw the meat away and put the grill iron on his truck, then drove off, deaf to her complaints. Another cook she had cause to remember was the one who produced about fifty rissoles — and that was all they got until they'd eaten the lot a few days later.

"What about that cook who used to steam the rib bones for supper, then grill the ones we didn't eat next day?" said Peggy.

"And how about his pastry?" Alice reminded her.

"How could I ever forget it!" Peggy replied. "Both me and sister Bub broke our teeth eating his pastry."

"Gawd, he was rough, that cook," Alice said, shaking her head.

Both Alice and Peggy agreed they did not consider that they had faced any great hardships either as they grew up in the Channel country, or later when they reared their own children in the bush.

Once, as they were mustering cattle on Durham Downs, a big rain came and their truck had to be left behind. So with two small kids hanging on behind, they tailed the cattle from camp to camp with pack horses.

"That lasted about three weeks," Peggy told me. "Trying to keep the kids dry, that was the worst. Yet them kids never seemed to get sick in the bush, only when they reached town."

"What about the time the kids ate the clover?" Alice put in.

"Oh yeah, that was after big floods in the Channel country and there was grass and clover everywhere. These little kids of ours — they weren't even two years old then — used to watch the cattle grazing around. They hadn't any toys, you know, there were only the horses and cattle to play with. Well, this day we watched those kids in that green, lush pasture, getting around on hands and knees and putting their heads down to feed like the cattle — I'm sure they thought they *were* cattle, because they were eating the clover and pigweed. Needless to say, they ended up with gastric, the runs. They cried all night, poor little things, and got kicked out of three different swags they dirtied."

"Yet we used to nibble at a lot of that stuff — wild spinach, crowfoot, pea bush, and we used to cook pigweed in the campfire ashes," Alice reminded her sister. "Of course, we never saw many green vegetables because we hardly ever saw a shop. We had no fresh fruit, no milk every day like we have now. Sometimes it was months before we saw a town, yet we never went hungry." She paused, recalling another incident. "One time, me and John and another old stock-man got caught in the rain as we travelled with pack horses, taking our horses to Planet Downs. We made it to a sandy ridge and camped there for three days. The ground was too boggy even for the horses. We only had a bit of flour left, and for those few days we survived on johnnie cakes and witchetty grubs."

They spoke of one meal they were not allowed to share. From time to time, different station camps would meet up for mustering, with Aboriginal stockmen and whites from all over camping close together. One day, some Aboriginal men had caught this huge snake, and that night they cooked it. The girls asked for some of it, but they were told by the old men: "You can't have 'em, this is men's tucker, can't gib 'em girls."

Sometimes tucker was not so easy to come by. Like the time Peggy, Alice and John watched some musterers kill a bullock beside a dam. "Then us three kids were left to cut it up, pack the meat on the packhorse and take it home," Peggy said. "The full pack-bags were too heavy for us to lift onto the pack-horse and we were too short to lift the meat high enough to fill the bags — so there we were, alone with all this meat. So eventually we led the quiet old horse up to the bank of the dam and carried the meat over. Then with Johnnie sitting on the horse's back atop the pack-bags, we passed up the meat and he dropped it into the bags, trying to balance the weight on each side."

Both the girls stressed that growing up mostly in the Channel country, they took a delight in meeting such challenges. They told me that the Channel country was like paradise after rain — the lushest natural grazing and fat-tening pastures in the world. But during drought it became a hellish, barren landscape, the formerly lush black earth a maze of widening cracks, so wide that at times a horse might break a leg just walking across the cracky ground.

Alice recalled that during their first trip droving cattle out of the Channel country, on their way to Bourke, Dad told them: "We cross the Paroo River today." They were expecting to see a big waterhole. This was at Hungerford, on the New South Wales–Queensland border. "Late that evening, as we drove the cattle onto night camp amid hopbush, mulga and sandhills, with the dingo netting border fence to one side, I said to Dad: "Well, where's that Paroo River?' — 'That's it, you came across it back there.' And he pointed to the tops of a few coolabah trees showing above the greyish mulga and green hopbush. — 'What, the culvert over that little hollow in the road?' — 'Yes, yes,' he said. 'That was the Paroo River.' "

Peggy went on with her story. "In 1958 we were mustering around Windorah, and we took a mob of cattle from Carevia Station to Yaraka. After that trip, Alice took off to Cloncurry and married Bill Fortune. I stayed in Yaraka, working at the pub, until my uncle Arthur Walton and my brother Johnnie came through with a mob of sheep — then I left the pub and went with them. We took the sheep to North Hampton Downs, then Johnnie and me caught a bus to Winton for the World Championship Rodeo.

"Meanwhile, Mum and Dad were on their way to Winton with cattle from Davenport Downs, and we went out to join them. We all spent Christmas that year in Winton.

"I married Kevin McKellar. He had his own droving plant — he was said to be Kidman's youngest drover. Our first trip together was from Yaraka to Windorah, and then he took cattle with his packhorse plant from Glengyle. I rejoined him at Beetoota and we went on to Durham Downs. I was six months pregnant at the time. We took the horses back to Windorah, and soon after I went to Charleville and had my first baby, Billy. There were other trips, from Durham Downs and South Galway into Quilpie, and from Davenport Downs to Winton. By then we had a truck. We spent much of our time fencing, and we had one spell on Monkira Station, with Kevin as cowboy and me as cook."

At Monkira, Peggy told me, there was an Aboriginal woman from Alexandra Station, in the Northern Territory. The boss's wife gave orders that she was to be fed outside the homestead. Yet when Peggy was away, that same Aboriginal woman was called in to help with the cooking for all the people because the mistress of the homestead was incapable of making her own bread.

I myself was aware of many similar situations: when no other labour was available, Aborigines were called on to cook the tucker. They were as clean as white cooks.

"Of all the jobs we took on," Peggy told me, "the worst must have been the time we went brumby shooting. I still remember the first brumby we shot. There were thousands of them running wild out there, and as we drove up to the animal we'd killed I felt sick. I thought, 'We've got to cut this poor thing up'. For all those years, horses had been so much a part of our lives. 'I can't do this,' I told my husband, 'I don't think we shoulda taken on this job.'

"So there we were, needing money, out in the Never-Never beside a dead brumby stallion, trying to come to terms with what we'd just done. After a lot of discussion and soul-searching, we decided, 'Well, we shot the poor bastard, so now we'll have to cut him up'. That was one job I hated, and we didn't stay in it for long.

"There were plenty of fencing jobs — by then we had a

tent, with beds and mattresses to sleep on. Kevin worked as a truck driver and council worker for a while. I recall that when we were out droving and fencing I used to make yeast bread and I'd let the mixture rise as we went from camp to camp. The same with my washing — the babies' dirty nappies were also done on the move. I'd fill a flour drum with warm water, put in some Rinso, and plunge them into it before we moved camp. They got jiggled up and down in the water on the rough dirt road, and at the next camp all I had to do was boil them up and rinse them. My clothes line was a fence, or the nearest tree or bush.

"You know, it's strange," Peggy said, "but when I was droving as a girl, then later when I went fencing with my husband and kids, I'd ride past homesteads and sometimes I'd wish, 'Gee, what I'd give to live in a house'. Yet when I got to live in a house, I found it was no fun at all — just a lot of cobwebbing, mopping floors and such. Even today I'd sooner live out in the open."

Peggy went on to tell me about some of the tragedies of her later life. First there was the break-up of her marriage, then the tragic loss of three of her four sons.

"Yes, I've had plenty of sadness," she said. "The loss of my children, and my Mum. And Dad. It may seem strange when I say that Dad was my worst loss, but he was … well, sort of a good old mate, and when I lost him I had no one to turn to, especially after the break-up of my marriage. He used to say, 'You can do it on your own, girl. But always remember I'm here'. He gave me strength to carry on." She sighed. "My son George was my saddest loss, because he always tried to keep us all together. They were all different sorts of tragedies — Mum, Dad and my sons."

I asked Peggy how she found life in general today.

"Well, it's a lot faster. I think people today are missing

too much, everybody rushing around looking at clocks. They haven't time to look at the countryside, trees, sunrise and sunset — things like that. You say to people, 'Isn't that a beautiful sunset' and they just look at ya in a silly way."

"Maybe they're looking for neon lights," I suggested.

Peggy laughed. "Yes, life has become pretty artificial, with no time to look at nature."

"What about politics?" I asked her.

"Well, today everybody seems to rely on someone else for everything — food, housing, the lot. And it seems as though they're incapable of fixing anything for themselves."

Today, Peggy is employed as a cleaner and stocker at Woolworths Supermarket in Mt Isa. She works two shifts, evening and morning.

Alice Bates Gorringe Fortune has recently retired from the Cloncurry Shire Council. She enjoys fishing, travelling over the old tracks and fossicking across the outback. And she showed me some rock which had fossils hundreds of thousands of years old embedded in it.

Alice has faced and overcome many challenges in her lifetime. The first was when she fled with her parents from the mission in New South Wales and an oppressive way of life. Then, together with her sister, she worked heroically in the droving and mustering camps. Alice and Peggy Gorringe were the equals of many of the stockmen, and often surpassed some of them with their skills.

"I started when I was nine and I left when I was twenty-two. I got married and raised six children," she said.

Alice has known the joys and anxieties of being a wife and mother, and today, as a grandmother living in retirement, another challenge looms ...

Ironically, in view of the recent Mabo Land Rights legislation, Alice is facing a claim from her white neighbour over part of her property, which includes her bedroom. It is a prolonged boundary dispute with both the neighbour and the Cloncurry Shire Council. Uneducated, with no one to turn to, and under considerable duress, Alice has been faced with signing away her backyard to preserve her house. She is still fighting what she considers an unjust white land claim over her property, and she is not about to give up easily. Alice might be described as the first Mabo casualty ... not over a "white backyard", a phrase the media have used so often in recent times, but over a white landrights claim over a black bedroom.

Wally Mailman

The Min-Min light and a miracle

In 1923, Gilbert Mailman was employed on a cattle station in the wild, rocky, tree-covered slopes of the Carnavon ranges, where today tourists flock to view the magnificent scenery. Throughout the ranges are sacred sites and ancient Aboriginal cave paintings, the Dreaming places of its people since the dawning of their history.

In June that year, Gilbert headed out of the ranges towards the town of Angethella, with his heavily pregnant wife. He followed the south-westerly course of the Warrego River, one of the furthest headwaters of the Murray River. These waters flow thousands of miles across the continent, to empty into the southern ocean. But as Gilbert urged on his tiring horses pulling the wagonette, I am sure his thoughts did not dwell on where the Warrego waters came from or where they went.

The sun dipped low and shadows spread from the coolabah trees lining the steep banks of Sawpit Creek. The weary horses jogged down to the sandy creek bed — and there disaster struck. As the horses struggled in the loose, heavy sand, to Gilbert's dismay the wagon pole broke. Sunset was fast approaching. He helped his wife down, then somehow managed to steer the wagon out of the creek bed. He set the horses free to graze and rigged his tarpaulin between the wagon and a coolabah tree. His wife was now in labour, and it was there, on 12th June, 1923, that Wally Mailman was born.

In later years, Wally's journey through life would take him much further afield than the wandering waters of the Warrego River. From his humble birth beneath the coolibah tree, he would achieve heights of recognition and respect as a bushman and drover, as a rodeo rider and judge in both Australia and New Zealand, and would shake hands with the Queen at the opening of the Stockman's Hall of Fame.

The story of how the Mailman family came by their name (Wally had four brothers and a sister) is intriguing. Wally told me that his great-grandfather was a Maori who had to leave his homeland in a hurry. On the boat from New Zealand, he became friendly with a Chinese called Long, and after he landed in Australia he took the name of Billy Long. He found his way to outback Queensland, and married into an Aboriginal/Indian family. "Lucy Long, Billy's daughter, became my grandmother," Wally said. "She married this German called Mueller — he was the packhorse mailman in the Carnavon ranges. They was my grandparents on Dad's side. Grandma had no education, like most others at that time. Well, it wasn't long before everyone who found the German name of the packhorse mailman too hard to pronounce began calling him "Charlie Miller" instead to simplify things. Then he became known as just "Charlie the mailman". Now Charlie Mueller, or Miller, otherwise Charlie the packhorse mailman, was often gone for days, sometimes weeks at a time, doing his rounds of the Carnavon stations, leaving Lucy and the kids to tend the spare horses and so forth. One time while Charlie was away on his lonely journey with the packmail, along comes one of them government men, lots of papers and stuff, wanting to know everything about this family." Here Wally looked at me. "You know this fella?" he asked.

"What fella?"

"You know — come to count the people."

"Oh, the Census," I said.

"Yeah, yeah, the Census — that's him. Anyway, he's asking Grandma, what's her name. But that old woman couldn't spell Mueller or Miller or whatever, and that government man can't understand Granny. — 'Well, how you spell your name, who are you? Whose kids are these?' — 'Oh, you know, Charlie the mailman, that's the father of these kids,' Grandma answered. — 'Charlie Mailman,' said the government man, scribbling furiously. At last he had a name — and this was how all of Lucy Long and Charlie Mueller's kids became little Mailmans."

On hearing this story, I recalled an episode from my own schooldays. My official name was Herbert Horsley Wharton and it was printed boldly on my schoolbooks — the first time I had seen my name in print. One evening after school I clearly remember crossing the gully and resting in the shade of a big old spreading coolabah tree. I looked at my printed name (I'd learned how to spell it by this time), and sitting there alone, I thought: "Horsley — what a silly bloody name," so then and there I simply changed it to "Morsley". Next day at school I pointed out to the teacher the spelling mistake that had been made when my name was recorded, and forever after I signed my name "H.M. Wharton". Even my birth certificate, which I applied for years later, was issued in that name. I had to tell the teacher: "Mum can't spell" — only late in life did she manage to laboriously sign her name rather than put an "X". I told no

one, but years later I found that the Horsley was from my
father's side of the family.

Back to Wally Mailman's story. He grew up in the bush
with limited education, taught mainly by his older sister,
who had herself been taught by the station manager's wife
and through correspondence school. The Mailmans had a
more or less permanent camp on Bogarella Station, living
in a hut away from the homestead. Gilbert had a paddock
for his own horses, some ten or fifteen of them. When
mustering was in full swing he would be gone for weeks,
even months. During the hot summer he would be employed digging wells in the sandy bed of the Warrego and
its tributaries. Bert, Wally's oldest brother, was often away
with his father, and as a result Bert picked up very little
education.

"I didn't get to be in the mustering camp like my older
brothers straight off. I went working for a well digger and
building cattle yards, and I became pretty good with an axe.
When we were camped near a mustering camp, a lot of
them older fellas taught me to make greenhide ropes. My
first job as a stockman was on Babbibora. It had just
changed hands and was being restocked by the new owner,
and they had bought a big mob of mostly unbroken horses
from all over the countryside, a real brumby lot they were.
Head stockman at the time was Fred Lawton, a now legendary stockman and horseman of that era. Fred began breaking in about fifty head of these horses, some of them real
mean old brumby types, and I became his offsider.

"It was a real hurry-up job, breaking them in. We'd run
them into a yard, rope them, choke 'em down, a bit of
bagging down and mouthing, then get 'em out of the yard
quick and into the mustering camp to be worked. Some of
them horses could really buck. I wanted to be a good rider

so badly that I got on everything they would put under me, and many a buster I had too! One morning I was thrown five times before I left the horse yard off this big mean old brumby. I still recall how I was thrown the fifth time, striking my head as I was tossed through the rails. I was knocked out. Later, while I lay there watching, still dazed, another Aboriginal stockman, Frank Geebung, got on the horse and when they opened the gate he went bucking across the paddock with Frank flogging him with his hat. He was another great horseman. After that I still went back looking for more rough horses to ride."

I remarked to Wally that in those early days he was laying the groundwork for a successful pro rodeo career. And I reminded him of the unwritten code of the West concerning stockmen's land rights claims: it was always said that anywhere in the bush a stockman was thrown, he could stake a claim to earth within a radius of six feet. I myself would own many acres if this were legitimate — and I know of others who could lay claim to millions of acres, great mates in the bush who would never become horsemen, no matter how hard they tried.

I sympathised with Wally and recalled my own early days as offsider for a wise old-timer who would urge me on, saying: "Come on, boy, he's a quiet horse, this one — I broke in his father and his grandfather too. He don't buck." Finally I would mount that quivering horse as my mentor held him by a twisted ear. Then — "Okay! You're right!" — and that quiet horse became a blurred ball of bucking fury until the ground came up to greet me and I lay in the dust. Then the old-timer would try to soothe the nervous tremors of that bloody horse in a soft, cooing voice, looking over his shoulder and saying: "I don't know what happened — he got a fright, you scared him, poor fella, he's still trembling."

I found this hard to believe, seeing that the horse was so much bigger than I was, and able to kick harder and bite. That old horseman would sometimes bring together an unbroken mount and a young stockman who had never ridden a wild horse. Both the stockman and the stockhorse were unknowingly being shaped by the wily horsebreaker. Back in the early days, there was always someone who wanted to become a great rider, ready to suffer the process of learning to tame wild horses and wild cattle. No doubt this was the way the sport of rodeo riding grew both in Australia and in America.

So the educating of Wally continued. At first, like the other accomplished riders, he used a small poley saddle — and went on staking his claims to land rights. Until one day Fred Lawton, probably despairing of his offsider's ability to stay on a bucking horse, showed him a big knee-pad saddle and fashioned a monkey strap for him. (This was a twisted or plaited strap used for mounting horses, fastened to the top of the knee-pad and used as a grip to hold on to when the horse bucked.) Once Wally was in this new saddle, Fred gave him some valuable advice on how to become a buckjump rider — "Get a grip on the horse with your legs, hang onto the monkey strap and learn to follow the horse when he's bucking. Once you learn this you're on your way. If you can't ride in this saddle you can't ride a horse."

After this Wally improved and busters became less frequent. Here I might add words of wisdom I've often heard given to a young, aspiring rider thrown off a bucking horse: "It's right, boy, you're a balanced rider, you only over-balanced that time." And to someone knocked almost unconscious after landing on his head: "Ah, you're learning to land properly now. Much better to land on your head, you save your riding boots, they don't wear out so quick. You're learning real good, boy!"

Thus Wally had his grounding, as you might say in more senses than one. He then worked as a horseman and stockman in the Carnavon ranges. One day he ventured further down the Warrego River to Charleville, and there he met up with another legendary horseman and horse-breaker, Harry Hawkins, who was looking for an offsider.

For the next twelve months Wally worked for Harry and learned from him. "He would handle the horses and I rode them," Wally told me. "My first job with Fred Lawton laid the foundations, but it was Harry who really topped me off. I had become cocky, full of confidence, by now. The station owner where we were breaking in the horses wanted to pay me boys' wages. But I insisted, with Harry's backing, that if I was doing a man's work then I wanted a man's pay. That was the first time I got men's wages. I was about seventeen. They were a bit funny in those days — station bosses didn't want to pay anyone much money, yet they couldn't do the jobs themselves. That is one reason I have always believed in unions. They was the only insurance against unscrupulous station owners and managers.

"I stayed twelve months with Harry. I learned to plait whips and belts and how to crack four whips at once — but how he balanced his whips I don't know. Harry had served in World War I, and he once cracked his whips before King George V, over in Palestine."

While Wally was with Harry, as well as breaking in the horses he attended a training camp for the citizen military force at Burrenbilla Station, six miles from Cunnamulla. As Wally said, this was supposed to be the very last line of defence against Japanese in their march south if they had invaded in 1942. Then he spent Christmas in Mitchell and went to work at Wombelbank Station, where his uncle was head stockman.

"How many cattle they run there?" I asked Wally.

"I don't know, but one year we branded six thousand calves. And that was the first time I seen the cradles used for branding calves. Before that they mostly used to scruff them or use a bronco horse." Suddenly Wally grinned. "It was funny — you know them old brumby horses me and Fred broke in on Babalora Station? Well, they'd been sold to Wombelbank. Old and mean they were, old outlaw horses. But there was some great horsemen working at Wombelbank and riding a buckjumper was all in a day's work for many of them. Eddie Smith was there — he was a great horseman too. I spent about two years at Womblebank and it was there I done the horse-breaking on my own for the first time. They were good days. We camped out most of the year, mustering."

One time at Womblebank there was a big rain and no one was able to drive or ride around — the ground was too boggy. The stockmen and sawmill workers got tired of reading books or playing cards, so some of them decided to build a raft and float down the flooded river to Mitchell. But they didn't get far: the raft was tangled up in some trees, and Wally said that one fella was drowned. "We had to scout around on either side of the flooded creek to find the body," he said.

It was while working at Womblebank that Wally got his first taste of rodeo, at a place called Charlie's Creek, at the foothills of the ranges. It was 1946. "You know," Wally told me, "I went there and competed, and fell in love with rodeo. From then on I wanted only to become a rodeo cowboy."

Wally's newfound love of rodeo, combined with his earlier determination to succeed as a rider simply by picking himself up off the ground after a buster as many times as it took was to be the basis of his success over the next forty years. During that period there may have been greater riders in the rodeo arena, but there was none more dedicated than Wally Mailman. Although small of stature, he was tough and wiry, and as well as riding buckjumpers and bullocks, he captured many bulldogging events, including a win at the Mt Isa rodeo.

At Charlie's Creek that day, miles from anywhere, Wally competed in the wild cow milking event and received a blue ribbon for his first-ever win. And that day, as he said, he fell in love with rodeo.

"For it is a romance," he said, "and it has lasted unabated to the present day." I can vouch for that, having known Wally for years. As a rodeo competitor he found success all over the eastern states of Australia and in New Zealand, competing against the top professionals on both sides of the Tasman in bullock riding, saddle bronc riding, bareback riding and bulldogging. Together with the legendary R.M. Williams, Wally was elected to the steering committee of the Australian Rough Riders' Association (ARRA), which paved the way for it to become a truly professional sport with protection for riders. Today this has grown into the Professional Rodeo Cowboys Association.

Wally was a popular contestant with his fellow competitors and the spectators alike. This was borne out after his retirement from riding, when he was made a life member of the PRCA and then became a professional rodeo judge, cracking his whip at rodeos held at such remote Aboriginal communities as Mornington Island, in the Gulf of Carpentaria, as well as Mt Isa — the biggest and richest rodeo in the land. For Wally, the honour of being asked to judge the nation's top riders is indeed an honour, but being asked to

judge at Mornington Island was a very special honour, and
the mementoes he received are treasured as highly as any
of the many ribbons and silver belt buckles he has been
given elsewhere, including the buckle he received as a
member of the official reception party assembled to meet
the Queen at the opening of the Stockman's Hall of Fame,
at Longreach.

From Womblebank Wally went back to mustering on Bab-
biloora Station. After the mustering was over one year, a few
young fellas were sitting around when one of them, Jim
Tutty, who was reading a paper, said: "Hey, they want some
drovers at Mt Sturgeon near Hughenden. What if I get a
plant together — will you fellas come with me?" They
agreed, and that was how Wally began droving.

"First we had to get some horses together," he said. "Real
brumbies they were — some were buckjumpers. Eventually
Tutty got enough horses and a wagonette and we started
out with the plant from Augathella to Hughendon, passing
through Tambo, Barcaldine, Muttaburra. After Hughenden we went on to Mt Sturgeon. We was breaking in and
taming the horses as we went. We was all youngsters except
for Billy Lawton, he was a bit older." Wally paused, then
asked me: "You know Claude Poncho?"

"Yeah," I answered.

"Well, he had just got married to Maudie Pickett. Maudie
became our cook and Claude was the horse tailer. On the
trip out we was still buying horses, and I recall I bought this
big piebald, a buckjumper he was, but with work he turned
out a real good stockhorse. I sold that same buckjumper
after we delivered the cattle, twenty-two weeks and two days
later, to two other famous horsemen, Bluey and Splinter

Bunyon, at Brewarrina. They were both noted rodeo pickup men, and that piebald became one of their pickup horses.

"That was my first droving trip. We took delivery of 1,000 head of cattle at Mt Sturgeon and came back through Augathella, where my brother Len joined us for the rest of the trip. Past Charleville we went down the Nebine into New South Wales, past Brewarrina and finally delivered the cattle at Dubray Station, near Warren. Altogether, that whole trip — getting the plant together, walking the horses out, bringing the cattle back, would have lasted well over six months. It would have taken even longer if we'd walked the horses back home, but we brought the droving plant back to Brewarrina and camped there for a few weeks, and then after the horses were rested, Jim Tutty decided to sell them — all the horses, the saddles, wagonette, the lot, rather than take on the long, lonely ride home."

I might add here that in them days, there were no decent roads and very little motor transportation of stock. The roadtrain was unheard of as yet. Drovers did the job of moving stock effectively and cheaply, working in conjunction with the railways, and that made everyone happy. Now the drover is almost obsolete and the railways, once the lifeblood of the inland, are threatened with closure. Today, heavy transport trucks exude polluting exhaust fumes for the sake of faster multinational profits. Men who would formerly have been stockmen and railway workers now repair the damaged roads, helping to shift the mineral and pastoral wealth further away from the people who helped to create it. And always at the bottom of the ladder are the Aboriginals — in terms of health, education and the wealth that flows from their one-time tribal lands.

While Wally was at Brewarrina, he went to a rodeo in

Walgett, and joined the ARRA. That was in 1947. "I got a second in the buckjump, as it was called then," he told me proudly. (Later, with the advent of Americanisms, this event became today's "Saddle bronc ride".) "I also tied for first in the bullock ride," he added. It was much later that bulls were used full-time at rodeos, and bull-riding became the most dangerous — and the most exciting — event of all.

"You know," Wally told me, "I went from there to Coonamble rodeo the next week. By then I was an addict, I was hooked on the sport." He paused. "Well, Tutty sold his plant and after that I went to Bourke to catch an aeroplane home to Charleville."

Wally recalled his first plane ride vividly: about to take off, the DC3 was delayed by a plague of grasshoppers on the runway. Eventually the moving mass passed on, the plane took off and arrived safely at Charleville — with what Wally still believes was a bad miss in one engine.

Soon after, he won the open buckjump event at Charleville Centenary Rodeo, and after a further spell on Womblebank Station he began to compete in rodeos as far away as Warwick. For years, Warwick was the top rodeo in Australia, and here Wally made the finals of the open buckjump event. In those days rodeo riders used little saddles and there were no soft landings — the arena was hard, slatey ground full of bindi-eye. The pickup men were real heroes.

In the 1950s, Wally worked for another Charleville drover, Claude Burns. He became his right-hand man, droving mainly from Caldervale Station at Tambo, taking mobs of cattle into the Walgett area of New South Wales. After delivery, Claude would head home to Brisbane for a break, leaving Wally in charge of getting the plant back to Calder-vale to pick up the next mob.

"They were good trips on the whole, each took around three months. Good cattle, too."

However, there was one droving trip Wally will always remember. This time they did not start out from Caldervale, but picked up a mob of 1,200 head of the wildest rushing cattle he has ever seen. Strange as it may seem, it was these very cattle that led to Wally's belief in God …

"Before I begin this story, I should let you know that I was baptised a Catholic, but didn't like church and didn't really believe in God or religion," he told me. "We took delivery of those cattle off the train at Yaraka, a small town not far from Blackall, and headed off for Quilpie. After a few days, them cattle were rushing day and night. They were truly the worst mob I have had anything to do with. They were terrible at night, they would take trees out by the roots as they rushed. Claude would warn us, 'Don't try to stop them straight off — if they rush at night, keep out from them and let 'em gallop for a while, then try to turn them. See what they gonna do first.' — Well, we were double-watching them this night and they took off, and there I am, lapping along out from them in the dark. But you could tell what they were doing just by the noise of them bellowing and timber cracking.

"This night, south of Yaraka, I was mounted on a pretty good horse, galloping along out wide, watching and listen-ing. I decided they had galloped enough, and it was time to bring them around and steady them. So I swung the long reins under the night-horse and he took off flat-out for the leaders of the rushing cattle. But a few seconds before we reached the lead, all of a sudden my hair stood up and I got this cold shiver. I said to myself, "What's wrong?" and I pulled the night-horse to an abrupt stop. A split second later the lead cattle hit this fence. Sparks flew off the wires and you could hear the fence posts breaking off as the mob stampeded on. Some were killed, some crippled. I pulled up shaking. If I had not experienced that strange feeling and had galloped on, me and the night-horse would have been crushed against the fence by rushing cattle — or else we would have crashed over the fence a split second before the cattle and been trampled to death as they rushed on. I believe God saved me that night. I didn't know that fence was there. Yes, God saved me. I got that there feeling just as if He spoke to me, and I pulled up. That's why I do believe in God. That was the most frightening experience I ever encountered. They were really bad, them cattle. They'd go mad, take off running, stop and start again. Next day we saw the devastation caused by that rush, the dead and dying cattle, one with a snapped-off fence post stuck through its stomach, many lame and crippled. — But all the same, a few more weeks and we got them cattle settled down and about three months later delivered them at Walgett."

Our conversation turned to the subject of racism. "Racism was always more evident in New South Wales than in Queensland," Wally said. "We'd be up the street after delivering cattle, might be eating chocolate or drinking lemonade, and the police would come along and say, "We don't allow you people in the pubs down here."

I myself can vouch for what I can only describe as the utter arrogance shown towards Aborigines by the members of the New South Wales police. For in that state, many Aborigines wanting to be what we described as "honorary white men" could obtain a dog tag, which to many was utterly degrading. Over in Queensland, we were barred from some pubs and served in others, but never did we apply for dog tags.

I recall one episode with an arrogant white policeman in Walgett — this was years after Wally's experience. I also went to the rodeo, and one night as I was standing outside a pub, with no intention of going in for a drink, along came this policeman: "You know you fella not allowed in pubs down here." To which I replied: "If I want a drink it will be up to the publican to decide if he wants to serve me or not." — After which I was accused of being "a cheeky black bastard", and it's possible I would have been arrested there and then but for the timely arrival of about a dozen other rodeo riders, black and white, who crowded around the young policeman. He then walked away, and the other riders asked me into the pub for a beer, but I declined — "Not now", I said, "but later." I stood there on that crowded street on rodeo night, wondering how such incompetent and arrogant people could have such power over others, and pondered on the fact that we were truly aliens in our homeland. With these thoughts in mind, I walked into the leading hotel and asked for a beer. Being New South Wales beer, I thought it tasted like horses' piss, but there I stayed drinking for the next hour, proving a point — if only to myself.

"While I was there, someone came in and said, 'Hey, that mate of yours, Roy —' (he was another great rider, a white bloke) '— a mob a' dagoes got him all bailed up outside the police station!' So around the corner I raced, and there, outside the police station, was my mate, clinging to a telegraph pole, his arms and legs wrapped around it. Four Greeks were trying to get him into the police station — evidently he had had a dispute with them in a cafe and a window was broken, but to me they were just four people trying to attack my mate and get him arrested.

"I simply said: 'What you bastards think you're doing with my mate?' They all began to yabber in their own lingo, fast and loud, but they let him go, and with them still yabbering and waving their arms we calmly walked back to the pub — and I might add that I swear the bloody beer tasted better after that! But shortly afterwards along came two of those Greeks and the young policeman who had earlier warned me about my non-rights in New South Wales, plus a detective. They took Roy away for questioning. Being a white fella, I thought he'd be okay. He just got a fine next day. So that was how I had my awful beer in a New South Wales pub without a dog tag or having to suffer the indignity of being an honorary white man. And this to me was a rewarding achievement in my fight for justice and equality."

Wally's story made me think of the previous generation before me, who paved the way to the stage we have reached today, through education and enlightenment, plus overseas pressure.

"Christmas 1959 I met up with another Aboriginal drover, Johnnie Nipps. He had delivered cattle to the trucking yards at Quilpie and wanted someone to take his horses, then spelling at Eromanga, back to Winton. I ended up working for Johnnie for quite a while, droving fat cattle mostly from the Channel country — Springvale, out that way. Between droving trips I would travel to rodeos. I also done trips with Fred Dollard and Pat Fogarty.

"That was just after big floods in the Channel country. Grass and water plentiful, cattle and horses fat and frisky. It was paradise droving those big, fat old Channel country bullocks. At night they'd lay down contented and full, and on cold wintry nights we could sometimes stand drinking coffee at the fire as we watched them."

These remarks of Wally's rang very true to me. I had worked for Johnnie Nipps myself — one of the best boss drovers I ever worked for, and despite arguments I also experienced easy trips droving fat Channel country bullocks. It was often said that the drover, if he so desired, would have been able to roll out his swag and sleep on the fat, broad backs of those bullocks. The cattle, full of grass, were quiet and contented. There were exceptions, though: some stations had a reputation — reasons unknown — for rushing cattle. Maybe it was the breed, but I believe it was man himself who somehow, down the line, had contributed to such unruly beasts, whether from breeding or handling.

Now Wally's thoughts turned to a favourite stockman's topic. "I'd often heard of the Min-Min light out in that country," he said, "and I told whoever was on watch at night to wake me if it appeared, but this never seemed to happen … Until one night, heading for the trucking yards at Winton, we camped just back from a waterhole near the Winton–Boulia road. A real cold, clear night it was, and Jacky Nipps (Johnnie's son) was on watch. I was in my swag, and he rode in and woke me, saying: 'Wally, you wanted to see that light — well, I just spotted it out there!' I jumped up to have a look but it was gone, it just disappeared. Disappointed, I went back to bed.

"We had a white girl, a jillaroo, working with us. About three nights later she done the second watch. Mrs Nipps was still cooking at the fire when this jillaroo rode into camp and, pointing to the road, asked: 'Is that the Min-Min light?' So I was woken and stood at the fire with them, the girl still seated on the night-horse. Together we watched the light coming towards us, just level with the highway ... 'Oh,' I said, 'that could be a motor car.' Once again I seemed to be denied my first sight of the elusive Min-Min light. We watched the car's headlights — as I thought — for a while, then it was my turn to go on watch. The jillaroo sat by the fire and talked to Mrs Nipps. Well, that light was still coming. It was a crystal-clear night ..."

I could well imagine such a setting in that country of open, rolling downs intersected by channels, with the night sky glowing with a million pinpoints of twinkling stars. Some, like Venus rising and setting, glittered and glowed so brightly that while you sat on the night-horse, you were tempted to reach out and capture a handful of that reflected light, seeming so near and yet in reality so far away.

This night, Wally rode around the sleeping herd expecting the car to pass by on the dirt highway. But when the light got about a hundred yards from the camp it turned off the road and headed into a broken channel ground where it was impossible to ride a horse, let alone drive a car.

"I thought: 'That's strange'," Wally told me. "And then I watched the light for a while, popping up and down amid that broken ground."

"Can you describe the light itself?" I asked.

"You ever seen them lights the old train guards used, walking along swinging 'em back and forth? — Well, that was how I saw that light. It would go dim for a while then brighten up. It was really bright when it passed near this big old coolabah tree on the edge of the channels near the cattle. It came so close to those sleeping cattle that I could see it illuminating the bark of that coolabah tree as it went past, bobbing up and down, back and forth amid that jumbled mass of broken ground. I became really concerned and went back to the campfire, to Mrs Nipps and the girl.

We all watched that light together as it circled around the camp, then away it went back to the highway. It was real strange. Next morning I looked at that coolabah tree and at the ground on its eastern side. There was no way a car or a man on a horse could have drove or rode through that mass of broken ground. Even walking you would have had to slide down the embankments on your backside and crawl up the opposite banks …

"Then I knew for sure I had seen the Min-Min light. All my life in the bush I had heard about ghosts and strange noises and sights, but now I realised the tales of the Min-Min light were really true. That was the closest I ever been in all my life to a spirit."

"You wasn't frightened?" I asked Wally. "What were your feelings as you watched the Min-Min light?"

"Oh hell, I had goose-pimples. But I wasn't as scared as I would've been if the light from the campfire and Mrs Nipps and the young jillaroo hadn't been there. I still had to watch the herd, but I was real quick to ride around and get back to the fire that night. You might say I was uneasy. And yet them resting cattle paid no attention to that light."

Wally told me that he saw the Min-Min light again, years later.

"It was when Cyclone Tracey hit Darwin, in 1974 — same year as the big flood in Brisbane. Rain flooded the inland too. I was living in Mt Isa then, and I'd taken my family home to Augathella for holidays. When we heard about Cyclone Tracey we packed up and hurried back over the mostly dirt roads that led across the miles and miles of black soil plains.

"A lot of cars got held up by rising floodwaters near the Ettna shearing shed, about twenty miles from Kynuna. They couldn't go forward, they couldn't go back — there were about twelve or fourteen vehicles in all. Some had families in them, like us, there was even a young baby. We all parked our cars back from the creek waters and then trudged across to the shearing quarters in the pouring rain. There were thirty-three people stranded at that shearing shed for three weeks. Food was dropped by an aeroplane flying low over the black soggy ground, but a lot of the food parcels busted open when they hit the ground. But we managed. Jane and I would give most of our tucker to the kids.

"Anyway, that's when I seen the Min-Min light for the second time. It was way back in the flooded channels — no one could walk or swim there, and no cars could move. I could see this light not far away, and after my experience all those years before, I knew straight away what it was. Well, the black ground was that soggy that when they decided to rescue us from the shearing shed by helicopter, it was too soft for the 'copter to land. We had to build a landing ramp out of rails and posts from an old sheep yard before we could be evacuated to Julia Creek.

"As we were being flown out, one woman asked the pilot, 'Could you fly over to where our cars are stranded? I'd like to pick up my suitcase.' — 'Oh,' said the pilot, 'we can manage that.' So we flew over the place where the cars had been left. Mine was the furthest back from the floodwater, and all we could see of it was the roof. There was no sign of the dozen or so other cars ahead of mine, they were completely submerged. So you can imagine the feelings of that woman and all the others on board that helicopter.

"From Julia Creek I caught a train to Cloncurry. The line was blocked from there, but the Army was there. I was working at Kalkadoon Park then and the Army had a camp there, so I was able to hitch a ride home in an Army truck. What should have been one long day's drive back home had taken six weeks, and my car lay waterlogged beneath the water, miles back. Later, when I went to collect it after the flood had gone down and the road had dried out, it was strange — you'd see these little creeks, with trees growing back from them, and you'd think that the floodwater could never reach up to this or that tree — then you'd look up into the high branches and the forks of them trees, and you'd see the bodies of sheep and other animals left high and dry by the receding flood."

After Wally's first encounter with the Min-Min light, he continued to travel around, going to rodeos from Mt Isa to Melbourne. He learned the butchering trade, and to supplement his rodeo earnings he worked in the meatworks during the week. At weekends he paid his entry fees for the pleasure of mounting an outlaw horse or wrestling a big, spiky-horned steer to the ground in bulldogging events. Sometimes he was rewarded with a little prize money, but mostly his "rewards" or souvenirs would be bruises, sprains or cracked bones. Yet that was the challenge that was rodeo: having been there and done that, I can attest to the great sense of achievement when you win.

In 1959, Wally went north to Mt Isa, not only to one of his biggest rodeo wins but to begin an association with that city that has lasted until the present day. For that year, the Rotary Club staged the first Mt Isa rodeo. The prize money was a meagre £500, with about a hundred riders competing. Today, the Mt Isa prize money exceeds $100,000 and over 500 contestants vie for the rich rewards. It now attracts visitors world-wide of all nationalities. At that first rodeo in the Isa, Wally won the bulldogging event and came second in the bareback ride against the best competitors Australia could muster. Since then, he has never missed a Mt Isa Rotary Rodeo, either as a competitor or as a judge. And for twenty years he was caretaker at the famous Kalkadoon Park, where the rodeo is held each year in August.

But before Wally settled in the Isa, in 1961 he ventured across to New Zealand (whence his great-grandfather had come all those years before). From his base in Hastings, where he was employed in the meatworks, he competed in five rodeos, and won the bareback bronc ride event at four of them. He became friendly with two New Zealand rodeo riders, Jacky Weepaki and Bruce Taylor, and they made plans to travel to Canada to compete in the world-famous Calgary Stampede. Through a Canadian school teacher who was a rodeo judge in New Zealand, they even lined up some work. The teacher's father, a rancher, promised them jobs and they would be able to use his ranch as a base.

"But I never got there," Wally said sadly. "That was one of my disappointments in life, I suppose, missing the chance to compete at the Calgary Stampede."

"How come you never went there?" I asked.

"Well, shortly before we were due to sail, I had this letter from my brother-in-law, back in Augathella. He told me they were getting this local rodeo affiliated with the Australian Rough Riders' Association, and he wanted me to take part in it. For four nights before the boat was due to sail from New Zealand to Canada I 'rocked on the bed', trying to decide between the plea from home and my desire to compete at Calgary. In the end my desire to see the success of the first pro rodeo in Augathella won out. Jacky and Bruce sailed for Canada without me — they're still over there, I believe."

Shortly after this, Wally retired from rodeo riding. He returned to New Zealand a few years later as a judge, and it was then he met his wife, Jane. They were married at Tokomaru Bay in New Zealand in 1964, and Wally brought Jane to live in Australia.

Wally has fond memories of his first tours of New Zealand, the country and its friendly people. He recalls how he and another rodeo rider, Bluey Wall, built yards and trapped brumbies in the shadow of the beautiful snow-capped mountains of Taranaki, in the King Country.

"Don't ever believe that all of them wild cowboys live in Australia or America — there's plenty of them in New Zealand," he told me.

For the next few years, Wally was employed in the Augathella district, handling horses and working on stations, including eighteen months as manager of Kennedy Station. His rodeo competition days were over, but he was in demand as a judge. And it was while he was judging at the Mt Isa rodeo one year that he got the chance to live in that city.

"By coincidence, the chute boss at the rodeo was none other than Jim Foote, the boss of Mt Isa mines. Somehow I mentioned that I'd like to settle in Mt Isa if a suitable job came up. — 'What you want, a job underground?' Jim asked. 'Lots of old stockmen working there.' — 'No, not underground,' I said. Then he told me that they intended to put up a caretaker-groundsman's cottage right there at Kalkadoon Park — so in 1969 Jane and me and the family moved in there."

He was employed at Kalkadoon Park for the next twenty years, helping to shape and care for the arena, in this way — combined with his judging — continuing the love affair with rodeo that began at Charlie's Creek, in the foothills of

the Carnavon Ranges, in 1946. He was also employed each
Saturday by the Mt Isa Racing Club as their swabbing
steward, a task he still carries out sometimes in retirement.
Wally is proud of his involvement with rodeo through the
years. He has seen it grow from a disorganised affair, with
no rules and without protection or insurance for the riders,
into the highly professional sport it is today, with the welfare
of both competitors and stock of prime consideration.
Today, the top bucking horses and bulls are held in as much
esteem as the nation's top riders who try to conquer them.

Wally could relate innumerable incidents he has seen at
Kalkadoon Park. After one rodeo, one cold August morning he and his fellow workers started to clean up the
ground. All around lay sleeping drunks, some with swags,
some without. They began to clean up the rubbish, empty
beer cartons by the score predominating. They approached
one pile of cartons, decided to burn them on the spot and
set them alight, then gathered up others to add to the pile.
Suddenly there was movement from beneath that great
heap of cartons and a man emerged, going crook about
being disturbed from his sleep. Wally still shudders to think
what might have happened if that drunk had not woken up.

Now living in retirement, Wally believes that life has been
good to him. He is still spry and fit-looking and enjoys a
night out at the club, with dancing and country music. He
lives happily with Jane in their house on a quiet, tree-lined
suburban street. Their children, now grown up, are making
careers for themselves which would have been unthinkable
for Aborigines in Wally's youth. One daughter is an electri-
cian, another an aspiring actress — Debbie has already
played a role in *One Woman's Song*, the stage adaptation of

the story of Oodgeroo of the tribe Noonuccal (Kath Walker). His two sons are both boiler-makers by trade, though one has now turned his hand to learning a chef's trade, in London.

"Good idea," Wally chuckled. "If that bloke can make a boiler and learn to cook in it as well, he'll never starve!"

Wally is a keen gardener, with a well-kept lawn, flower-beds, vegetable patch and fruit trees. He and Jane have two grandchildren who often come visiting. Sometimes Wally holds fears for the future of his grandchildren: it seems to him that alcohol and drug abuse and crime are getting worse, not better. We discussed these issues, and Wally found himself in a minority — both Jane and I agreed that the future holds more promise for all people. Today, drug abuse and crime are being properly addressed, whereas in the past the only solution was to place Aborigines in insti-tutions. Today we have equal rights and justice, and igno-rance and arrogance are being replaced by education and acknowledgment of the truth.

As we talked, sitting together in Wally's house, Boots, his old blue-heeler cattle dog, began to bark.

"What's up?" I asked.

"Oh, it's only the postman," Wally said. "That's the bark Boots gives when he arrives each day. You'll see, the dog will take care of the mail."

Moments later there was the sound of pawing and scratching at the screen door. Wally opened the door and took the letters from Boots's mouth. Then he told me how he had trained Boots to pick up pieces of paper when he was at Kalkadoon Park. "I always seemed to be walking over and over that huge ground to retrieve the papers the wind blew everywhere. It didn't take long for Boots to become a master of the game. I'd say, 'Get it, Boots!' and off he'd go. He must have saved me miles of walking."

It was time for me to leave and we went into the street, accompanied by Boots. There Wally spotted an empty wine cask lying in the gutter of that otherwise neat and tidy street. "Go fetch it, Boots!" he said, and immediately away went Boots, picked up the offending rubbish and brought it to his master, who placed it in the garbage bin.

I headed off to begin writing this tribute to a man who years ago had realised he would have to learn to become a great rider the hard way, unlike those few who were naturally gifted horsemen — and attained his dream to become one of the top rodeo riders in Australia and New Zealand.

Jack Guttie

Strange things happen on bush racetracks

"Where you born?" I asked Jack Guttie, a short, active, humorous man always ready to swap a yarn or a joke with his many friends.

"Well, I was born under a coolabah tree near Innamincka on 6th April, 1932, but paperwork say different. I remember happy days as a kid, plenty to do. Old people take us kids hunting — we had to do what we were told. The idea they was punching into our heads was that if we got lost somewhere we could survive, live off the land, keep going. What to eat, how to stop your tongue swelling when there's no water, getting duck on a big wide waterhole, putting bushes on your head and drifting close up. All them things. I got into trouble once real bad. Us kids decided it was easier to get eggs from the fowl house at the station homestead than find bush tucker. We got a big hiding. That was our schooling.

"Dad was a stockman on the station and Mum owned nine camels given to her by an Afghan camel man when he retired. Sometimes they used them camels on the station. When it rained, plenty of water everywhere, but come hot weather, surface water dries up — cattle stranded a long way from any permanent waterhole. That's when they used the camels, to get the cattle back to permanent waterholes. There wasn't many waterholes, they relied on windmills and dams.

"Well, Dad had a row with the station boss and pulled out. He went droving and me, Mum and the camels went with him. First we rode on one camel, then Mum led the pack camel and the others followed. She was the drovers' cook. I remember our first trip was from Glengyle. Dad got hurt there by a chestnut horse called Bulla. Mum would put me on the pack camel with the dough and yeast she'd mixed for bread in a dish. The idea was to let it rise on the way to the next camp. Well, one day this old camel got up real fast and me and the dish of dough ended up in the dust."

"What about the horses and camels — how'd they mix?" I asked Jack.

"Oh, the drovers' mob of horses didn't bother about the camels after a while. Only a strange horse would take fright. That trip was the first time I learned to ride on my own on horseback. I think they may have just put me on and drove me along with the loose horses. No more camel rides for me after that! When we finished that trip we came back up Coopers Creek, Durham Downs, Tanbar. I could ride good then on a horse. I clearly remember that Yamma Lake was dry and we cut straight across it — thirty miles we went that day with the horses and camels. About halfway across we pulled up for a rest, sitting in the shade of our horses. It was eerie — you couldn't see anything on the dry bed of the lake, it was a landscape with no features, not even a tree. You couldn't see where the shore started or ended. There was nothing but mirages and a big purple, bluish hill straight ahead. The landscape danced and weaved about us. Strange, that was. When we did get across they had to draw up water from a well with buckets for the horses. The camels were okay.

"After that we ended up at Planet Station. Dad and this drover was brumby-running and that's where I got my first horse, a chestnut brumby foal — but I could never ride him, he bucked too much for me. By then I had a pair of riding boots, but they was much too big for me. So I had a too-large pair of riding boots and a horse I couldn't ride.

"The next trip I recall, we took a mob of cattle from Morney past Innamincka. Some young bloke got drowned there, helping to swim the cattle over the river. We delivered the cattle at Quinaby, in South Australia. Then we went to Morney again and took another mob to Naryilco Station. By then I was galloping everywhere on my horse. We come back to Arrabury Station, and I recall mucking about there for a while, staying with my Uncle Bill and Aunty Alice. That's where I remember the last big corroboree. They came from Cordilla, Birdsville, Durham, Nappa Merrie, Nockatunga … It was the last time I danced there. All them old men was there, all painted up. Musta lasted a week. The boss and them from the homestead would come down at night and watch. That was sheep country then, I remember them taking wool away with two donkey teams.

"By then my mother and father had parted. She stayed with this old drover, old Joe, and went to J.C. and stayed there a while, and this old woman tried to teach me a little bit, but I got nothing out of it — ABC, that was as far as I got."

I smiled as I heard Jack mention "J.C." I thought that city people out there might wonder what on earth the initials stood for. And, if they heard a mob of bushmen talking about a trip to Canterbury, maybe they'd assume they were off to the Sydney racetrack of the same name. They'd be wrong ...

In far south-west Queensland, a mudbrick wayside pub once stood on the road between Windorah, Beetoota, Bedourie and Boulia. In earlier days it was an important watering place for people and for cattle; beside the pub the government bore and windmill was set amidst the gravelly, mulga-red ridges and spinifex hills. The site was officially gazetted as a township, and one John Canterbury came to survey and map the dusty streets. I have heard that J.C. stands for that surveyor. But another version has it that those are the initials of a member of the Costello family, which lived in the area. And yet another story tells of a group of travellers who, coming upon this so-called township, simply shook their heads in disbelief. "Jesus Christ!" they muttered, and hastily headed back east.

I know that the pub flourished for some time, and people camped around it over the years. The J.C. cemetery attests to some who lived and died there, including the young housemaid who fell pregnant and hanged herself in a back room of the pub. Her ghost was said to haunt the place.

Today, J.C. is the unofficial name of that unpeopled township of Canterbury — and the windmill is the only thing left standing, close by the remains of the pub. The bitumen beef road passes between the windmill and the mudbrick rubble and giant roadtrains go whizzing past, carrying cattle to the Quilpie railhead. A few miles further west lie the Morney Plains, inhabited by the fierce snake, the deadliest in Australia, more lethal than the taipan. Memories, windmill, ruined pub and cemetery are now the only reminders of the town.

All the surrounding countryside is part of Waverney Station, breeding place of the wildest and spookiest cattle a drover could encounter. And it was the owner of Waveney Station who brought about the demise of the J.C. pub. For there was trouble with the stockmen who mustered around it. Some would find their way to the pub, stay boozing for the rest of the day, and then, try as they might, they could never find the track that led away from the place. So the men went on drinking while the cattle ran wild. The station owner solved the problem quite simply by buying the pub and then closing it down. (Today, the station homestead no longer stands on Waveney — the property has been taken over by a pastoral conglomerate, and is managed from afar.)

Recently, I camped beside the windmill at J.C. on a wintry, moonlit night and listened to the dingoes' mournful howls. I thought of the child who once lived at J.C., who wandered away and perished. His body was said to have been partly eaten by dingoes. And cold south wind blew the bushes into shrouded shapes and rustled the silvery mulga leaves, and then I imagined the restless ghost of the young girl who hanged herself, and the spectres of long-dead stockmen on their phantom horses, come to pelt stones at the rubble of the pub until it turned to dust, cursing those who founded a town that never became, and a pub which had no beer …

But it is time to return to Jack Guttie's childhood on the stock route. After staying at J.C., he set off with his mother and old Joe on another droving trip.

"Mum still got her camels and old Joe his horses, and we took cattle from South Galway through Eromanga and Thargomindah to Bourke, in New South Wales. That was the first time I remember having some money, because I went up to this pub at Fords Bridge and bought a packet of Ardath cigarettes. Oh, I thought I was a full-blown ringer then, a big cattleman! But them old fellas sometimes put the whip on me, let me know I knew nothing. It didn't go astray on me I don't think.

"Well, when we got to North Bourke we have to get across the Darling River. Real wide, it was. So they pays someone who has quiet cattle to lead our mob across the big, old, high wooden bridge. It was a long way across, with a big curve in the middle. Gee, that bridge rattled as them cattle began to trot across! Well, we get across and out of the Channel country and then, you know, there's a big open plain and you can see the meatworks and trucking yards a few miles away. I remember, when we got out on that big plain, I could see this smoke and something going flat-out. It was a train, like a big snake with smoke coming out. I was fascinated by the sight — first train I ever seen. I wanted to get a closer look, but they told me it was a couple of miles away across the plain, headed for Sydney.

"On the way back with the camels and plant horses I got chicken-pox and ended up back in Bourke hospital. When I got better I stayed in Bourke for a while and had a good look at them trains. Then I got a ride back to Hungerford, where Mum and the drover were on their way back to Bourke with another mob of cattle and a couple of men. So I headed back to Bourke again. This time they swam the cattle over at the big bend in the river and walked the camels and loose horses over the bridge. We was using pack camels all the time. After that trip I remember real well, this old boss drover bought me this beautiful kid's saddle. And I remember getting this parcel all rolled up. I unrolled it and it was the biggest bag of boiled lollies. That was my wages. Oh, I thought I was made, I had these lollies, a new saddle, riding boots and a new hat — yes, I reckoned I was really a full-blown ringer now.

"On the way back with the plant we camped one night at Yantabulla, in New South Wales, and we was there all next day looking for the pony I rode, which had strayed. But we found it. Well, this policeman noticed me and he told the drover and Mum I gotta go to school, he'd havta take me in to get my schooling. He said he'd come down to get me in the morning — 'Don't go anywhere,' he warned. Well, we had no motor car, so he didn't suppose we could get away. But after supper Mum packed some tucker on an old horse and with me on my pony we took off. We rode all night (me in my new saddle), watching out for car lights on the road. Before sunrise we was back through the border gate at Hungerford into Queensland.

"We went over the Paroo and camped, laying low in the creek for a couple of days. Then two old drovers came along with camels and horses. Well, them two got on the grog there — I remember sitting down near the pub with a big brown bottle of lemonade, watching them have a fist fight. A policeman came and locked them both up until they were sober. Afterwards they were still mates.

"My oldest brother was with us on our next trip. We went from Morney to Naryilco, then we took a mob from Palpara to Durham Downs. It was a good life, droving. The next year we went to Keeroongooloo and settled down for a while on a station while we took four mobs to Quilpie trucking yards. The first time we went into Quilpie, Mum took me to Charleville and I had my first train ride! I met up with a mate at Charleville. This was during the war, you know, and there was lots of Yanks and soldiers about. I recall how me and my mate went walking around the streets picking up these things the soldiers used at night, rubber things. We used to blow them up and bang! they'd go off like a balloon.

Then someone told us what they was used for. It left a funny taste in our mouths for a while.

"In 1944 — I would be twelve then — we had Christmas at Windorah, then Mum went on droving with old Joe. My father was now head stockman on Keeroongooloo Station. He come and got me and took me into the mustering camp there. Five shillings a week — that was my first wages. I was on the book and by the end of the year I was paying tax — I was getting ten bob then, and plenty of damper, cornmeat and black treacle. When we finished mustering at the end of the year, me and Dad went to Malagarga Station. We went to J.C. that Christmas, travelling with a packhorse. Mum had left the camels there and we had to shift them, so we come back to Durham Downs, then took the camels to Arrabury Station. There were only five camels left by then and we let them go. They was finished and we left them to die or whatever.

"That's when Mum said she had to take me back to show me where I was born and what had been left there for me. When we got there, back near Innamincka, we met some relations and Mum said, "Son, that where you born, under that big old coolabah tree. When you grow up you gotta come back to get things left here for you in special place. I can't tell you about it yet, but later on, when you grow up, I'll show you.' Well, she never did take me back or mention them things again, not until years later, the night before she died in Charleville hospital. By then I was married, and my wife took our twins up to see her. Mum told her to give me this message, that I gotta go and see about what was left for me near Innamincka. But I never went.

"While we was at Malagarga we took a couple of mobs into Quilpie, then ended up mustering on Quartpot Station, Eromanga. Them horses all belonged to Durham

Downs. After we finished mustering, me and Dad took the horses back to Bundeena, then went to Noccundra, and we worked on Durham until about 1947.

"What about cutting off the tucker that was handed out?" I asked Jack, recalling an experience he had related to me.

"Oh, that happened to me on Morney, and I seen it there on Durham too. Sometimes you'd get tucker handed — more like chucked — out and other times the white cook would cut ya tucker if you sat with mates. I wasn't with Father then, I was on me own. Lotta them black fellas they had there under the Aboriginal Act worked for nothing, almost. The policeman out that way got them to put their fingerprint on paper for what little money they did have. And not long after, a lot of them old fellas were taken away to the mission." Jack shook his head. "Yet I ended up cooking meself on Durham for black and white alike, and let everyone help themselves. But I didn't like that job — mustering was the best.

"I remember, Leslie Thompson and Danny Grey used to put me on bucking horses and give me a belt under the ear if I fell off. I wasn't game to tell my father, but them fellas taught me to ride a buckjumper and throw a micky. I remember one day they threatened to belt me under the ear and made me get off to this young cleanskin bull — he had no horns. Anyway, this cleanskin knocked me down and blew snot all over me while them fellas looked on laughing. That was how I learned to be a stockman and a horseman."

I remarked to Jack how, with a few exceptions, most great stockmen and horsemen out there were Aborigines. He agreed. "I've got a lot to thank them old blokes for," he said.

"What about them days — were they good or bad?" I asked.

"Oh, they was good," he replied. "I took it all as part of learning. Discipline was the main thing. At night around the campfire, I could talk up sometimes, but I was mostly seen, not heard. We made our own fun, running, jumping, always trying to outdo each other. I suppose we wanted to learn to be better than the rest every time, whether it was riding a bucking horse, throwing a cleanskin or catching calves at branding time. We also made greenhide ropes." He paused. "I remember my father having a big argument with the station manager about this time, concerning me and a couple of young white fellas my age — I'd be fourteen or fifteen then. We had to go out before dawn, find and unhobble about eighty horses, ride buckjumpers, do the work of men. 'They must get men's wages, they doing a man's work,' my father said, so we got full pay for the first time."

From my own experience of mustering, I knew that station managers hardly ever came near the men in the mustering camps in them days. Everything was left in the hands of the head stockman. The manager rarely got on a horse.

Jack went on with his story. "I nearly got drowned in that country. I was crossing a channel when my horse suddenly went mad — he started plunging about in the water. By then I was in the water, and that horse came at me as I was washed downstream. Danny Grey saved me that time. He threw out his whip handle and dragged me in, then managed to get my hat — it had been carried two or three hundred yards downstream.

"But there were real lighter things that happened, too. Like the time Danny cut his foot, and as he was resting,

camped under a tree, a big carpet snake fell onto him. Or
one time when we just finished moving camp and everyone
was relaxing and laying around. Old Tommy Norman,
laying on his swag, was holding the fork of his loose-legged
khaki trousers. 'Boy!' he yelled out, 'undo the buttons on
my trousers, bloody snake up my trouser leg!' — 'Yer, a
bloody big black one!' someone yelled, and we all laughed.
But there was a snake up his trouser leg and he had a grip
on its head. Well, his buttons were undone and the trousers
and snake thrown away.

"That same year, Jack Boggs took delivery of a big mob
of bullocks at … I can't recall the name of the water-hole,
but it's still there, near the old bronco yard. Anyway, the day
before Jack Boggs arrived, I remember getting horned by
a mickey in the arse. All of us was there, yarding up to brand
these cleanskins. Well, that mickey broke away and of
course I took after him. The poor bugger, I didn't want him
to go back in the yard, I wanted to give him a go — I wanted
to roll him out on the flat, see. Anyway, I grabbed him by
the tail all right, but then I slipped and lost it and he spun
around and horned me fair in the arse, blowing snot and
snorting. I picked myself up and ran away. He musta stum-
bled, and I managed to get to this little tree, and there I
am, hanging on — can't climb any higher — and this
cleanskin, he's giving it to me, butting me up the arse.
Frightened the shit out of me. — Well, Danny Grey came
along and threw the bloody thing." Jack laughed. "I wonder
if Danny still remembers that. But anyway, we done that
mickey, we put the Durham earmark on him and you know,
cut him, and let him go. That's all I wanted to do and that's
all Danny wanted to do. But then Danny give me a bit of a
shaking up. He said: 'It's a wonder you weren't killed, doin'
a thing like that, you stupid bloody bastard.' We both

laughed then. 'So you wanted to be a big-gun stockman and show 'em?' he asked me. I wanted to show them all right — and if the truth was told, Danny was the fella that used to egg me on to these sorts of things.

"He was pretty good to me, Danny, he showed me all he could. But I tell you, he was a bit rough at times. I saw old Danny recently, we were sitting in the afternoon sun and I said to him: 'Gee, you were a bit rough on me.' There were some kids there with us and I told them: 'If your father was rough on you like Danny was rough on me — well, you might be pretty good kids.' "

Jack told me it was on this trip that Jack Boggs' horse tailer was drowned. "Bloody bullocks swam across the river and he went after them. The water was a fair depth and apparently he couldn't swim a stroke. He was only a young man. I don't now whether they buried him at Noccundra or Noccowelah, or maybe his parents might have come and shifted him. But I was the one who had to ride in the next morning to Noccundra. That was the place where they are now getting oil or gas or whatever. Old Tommy Norman — he's dead and gone now, but he was one of the real great stockmen out there — he said: 'Boy, catch your best horse.' I got to Noccundra late afternoon and reported the drowning at the police station. In those days the only pedal radios were at Durham Downs and the police station. Then I stayed the night with Jacky Lantern and his missus and rode back to camp next day."

"How far was that ride?" I asked Jack.

"Oh, you'd be looking at thirty-five or forty miles."

Jack resumed his story. "By the end of that year I was well up, I'd become an all-round stockman. After that — 1948, it was — we went to Charleville, then Quilpie and Durham. We spent the New Year at Eromanga with a bloke called

Danny Condon and some other fellas, we all camped there. Then we went to Kyabra, an out-station of Thylungra, a real big place." (Thylungra Station in them days was probably the biggest sheep station in Australia, running hundreds of thousands of sheep.) "My father had lined up this job, we were lamb-marking there. We marked about 10,000 bloody lambs at Kyabra, as well as mustering for shearing. And that same year we mustered 10,000 weaners at Kyabra and delivered them to Thylungra.

"Tell me how you mustered the sheep, Jack," I said, intrigued how in them days, before motor-bikes or helicopters were used for mustering, men could manage to ride so far on horseback, muster a 200,000-acre paddock and get home, all in the same day — and repeat the process until the muster was finished.

"Well, when we started to get ready for this muster, me and Freddy Dawson took spare horses and left them at the boundary riders' huts, six or seven horses at each place. My father was at one of them places, and old Charlie Conway was at Quartpot shed. It all sorta linked up. — Well, we set out in early morning darkness, with twenty-seven miles to go by road before we began mustering. We had twelve miles on that lap, and my father met us with the first change of horses — it was about five o'clock. From there we galloped up to the stony country, where old Charlie Conway had the next change of horses. He brought them from the shed and looked after the others until our return that evening to change horses again. We got another change at Harkaway. I can't think of the old fella's name there, but he had a wife and a fair lump of a daughter. I used to have my eye on his daughter, so I was glad to get to Harkaway."

"How old was the girl?" I asked Jack.

"Oh, she was about sixteen, a wadgin, but I had my eye

on her anyway. Yeah, you know I was fairly good-looking then and a bit smart."

"You polish your riding boots the night before?" I asked.

"Yer, oh yer, but I never had time that day to see her, I could only look at her and give her a smile. Well, we mustered there, turned them sheep over to that old fella, changed horses, then galloped back to old Charlie, changed there and again at my father's hut. We got home about nine or ten that night, had a feed and went to sleep. The next morning the horse tailer had the horses ready and we did another lap out and back. We done that for three days straight, big gallops to get there, then after the further-est part of the paddock was mustered — we got back a bit earlier. But we could do it, and we did — it was all interesting, you know, when I look back on it now."

"They'd be flat-out doing that muster even today with their motor-bikes, considering that country and the huge paddock, all stony hills and mulga," I remarked. "You fellas might have beat the sun when you got outa bed in the morning, but it sure beat youse to bed at night."

"That's right," Jack agreed. He paused. "Outa all the fellas that was with us that time, I'm the only one left now … no, I'm wrong, old Tommy is still alive." He went on: "Anyway, I remember when we was mustering for the shearing, me and Freddie went out and camped at my father's hut, and we found this opal in the rockface. It was a rainy day and the sun came out and was shining on it. I was too busy to do anything about it — I just took a few samples. But me and my family went out there in 1976 and got some more samples and sold them.

"After the shearing that year, me and Freddie worked at training some horses for a fella who lived round that way. When the time came round for the Flying Doctor race

meeting we walked these horses from Kyabra into Eromanga. We also brought in another couple of racehorses
belonging to a fella by the name of Stan Young. One was a
horse called Canteen. He was a good horse.

"I didn't know what was going on, I never had any
experience riding at races, but they put me up on Canteen,
and I'm the only Murrie sitting up there with Willie
Costello, Harker Conquest, Teddy Mead ... all those fellas,
riders like myself. The owner found it hard to get any
money on Canteen. Well, when they put me up on this
horse they said: 'Don't you win. If you let this horse win we'll
boot you up the arse.'

"Anyhow, we're off and racing, and coming around the
corner, Canteen is getting the better of me, starting to go
to the front, so I dropped the neck reins, put my foot
through the reins and of course that jerked the horse back
out. I didn't know I was doing wrong. The steward was back
at the start, and the rest of the field raced around me. And
this mare Lemon won. Of course, when I came in they asked
me about it straight. 'Ooh, you pulled that horse, didn't
you?' Mrs Sullivan said. I said I never, I dropped my reins
over my riding boot and my foot got caught, see, and the
horse was jerked up. That was my excuse.

"The worst part was that I found out my father had put
a lot of money on my horse. He was very disappointed that
Alfie and the others in the know never went and told him
— 'Listen, you gotta put the money on Lemon, don't back
that son of yours, he's not gonna win.' I suppose they
thought he was just an old fella walking around with a few
beers in him, you know. But the others all got their money
on that mare, a brumby from Thylungra Station."

"And how much you get out of that?" I asked Jack.

"Nothing. I never got nothing. A few years later I ran into

Alfie when he was droving and I told him: 'You're a nice
sort of bastard. My old father backed that horse I rode at
the races that day and I nearly got thrown off the racecourse
for the rest of my life — and I never got a cent out of it!'
But we didn't fight over it. I remember that I did get a big
bottle of lemonade after I won the blackfellas' race (that's
what they called it then). It was the last race and I won it on
Lemon, that same horse that beat me earlier. There was
Pilate Dockety, Charlie, an old fellow with a moustache …
I flew past them all when I won that last race. I was happy
I'd won — I rode a winner after all." Jack smiled as he
remembered. "It was fun, only a flat graded racetrack,
pretty dusty, a few rails in the straight on one side. No
barriers or stalls — just a man with a rag and that was it.
When he said 'Go!' you went, and if you was slow away or
your horse started bucking it was just too bad, it was your
blue."

And he added: "It's just like yesterday, all these things
that happened."

"Until 1949 I was still under my father, he told me where I
could and could not go. I was working around Windorah
yard-building, then doing windmill work with Len Dare. He
taught me all about windmills — he was a pretty good man
to work for, Len Dare.

"Then my father said I could get out and go and work
wherever I liked, so I had many jobs. In them days there was
no such thing as no work on offer.

"In the 1950s I got a job droving with Harry Gorringe.
We took 1,200 head of cattle with a pack-horse plant from
Mt Leonard Station down into South Australia. We ended
up near Marree, then came back to Arrabury Station and

picked up 600 fat bullocks and headed for Quilpie. This turned out to be the worst mob of cattle I have ever seen. After we crossed the Cooper channels and got into sheep country they started rushing day and night. I remember one night they rushed near a fence — they rushed through that fence backwards and forwards, from one side to the other. It was terrifying, and there were many left dead and crippled before that trip was over. Gee, we were glad to get that mob into the trucking yards at Quilpie and get some sleep!"

I might add that at this time, Quilpie was one of the biggest cattle-trucking centres in Australia, if not the world. Across the railway line, just a few hundred yards away, stood three pubs, a bank and shops, where some drovers ended up squandering their hard-earned cheques.

Jack did work with sheep droving for a while. He recalled his first visit to Winton with another Aboriginal drover, Arthur Walton, and 4,000 sheep from near Quilpie. That trip took about three months.

"One consolation with sheep droving was that each night the horse-tailer would rig up a rope break or yard for the sheep, so that unlike the cattle drovers, we was assured of a good night's sleep."

He smiled as he recalled another memory. "One of the few times in my life I became lost was in Winton. We rested the horses there for a day and I went into town. Well, when I tried to find our camp again that night — no hope! Everywhere I headed there was only these bloody prickly trees. I couldn't walk or even see through them, and eventually I waited until sunrise and then found the way back to camp."

I myself had seen Winton when it was engulfed by those strange trees — some sort of mimosa, I believe. Alien to the landscape, they had overgrown the town. Once Winton had been a small outback town in open country surrounded by a few coolabah trees growing in mostly dry watercourses, and a few mulga trees. But someone must have introduced this alien tree, and as I myself saw when approaching Winton in them days, they completely hid the town for a mile or so round about. This was another experiment with an introduced species gone painfully wrong — as many who tried to walk through that prickly forest would attest after having those painful poisonous thorns stuck into them.

Jack continued: "After that trip I went to Woorabinda to see my sister. She and the other children was taken away in 1950 — they just bundled them up and sent them off. They could have been playing up, but whether they were or not, they just sent you off to a mission in them days.

"But all up, it wasn't a bad life. Discrimination was always there, but my father made sure I got paid the same as everyone else when I started to grow up. In some places they would cut the tucker and serve you on the woodheap. I remember once, Dad sent me to work at Morney, saying 'You'll learn something there'. Anyway, I was the only Murrie there and they put me outside to eat on my own. When Dad found out he came over and said, 'You can't stay here'. That was a bad habit they got out of years back in that part of the country. In general, we were taught to mix with all sorts of people.

"One incident I recall way back was my mother giving me a hiding for being cheeky to the manager's wife. I tried to explain how the woman was abusing Aborigines like us all the time, but she didn't believe me — until one day she heard this woman going on, and then she gave the manager's wife a hiding with the broom."

Jack paused, then said thoughtfully: "I can honestly say

that I played a part in developing the country's pastoral industry, helping to install water facilities, yards and many other things."

"In 1965 I got married. It took a month to get the right papers because, like many other Aborigines of that era, I wasn't registered. Anyway, I finally got the papers that said I was born in Innamincka, so I came in from the station where I was working on a Thursday, fixed up all the papers that day, got drunk on Friday and married on the Saturday. Then I returned to work on the back of the mail truck on the Sunday.

"After that I started work on the relay gang in the railway. That was more or less the end of my days as a stockman, drover and windmill expert, for the children began to arrive — eventually there were seven. I was stationed at Wyandra, and ended my last five years of work on the railway as a ganger, until I resigned and moved to Cunnamulla, the place I still call home.

"At Cunnamulla I was employed as an alcohol counsellor, and that taught me a lot about being tolerant with others. Those were good years in my life … until 1986, when I lost my wife. Then for a while I experienced a real down period in my life. I could not accept the death of my wife for a long time, and I lost my way. But eventually, with the help from my family and many other people I got back on the right track. After that — well, the kids grew up and drifted away."

A few years ago, Jack met his present wife, Barbara, on the railway platform at Roma Street station. They were married in 1993. Today, Jack teaches his Aboriginal language, a language almost lost, and is still interested in the welfare of others. As he said, "Overall, I've had a pretty good life. Oh, I've had my ups and downs, I've seen a lot of unjust things happen in the past treatment of Aborigines. But there were a lot of people, both black and white, who done good by me, and they never had the recognition they deserved. There were good and bad people out there, and all of them taught me to look after myself.

"I was reared with all sorts of people and I had a lot of teachers in my life. Danny Grey, for instance — he taught me how to ride a rough horse and how to use my fists out on the grass. Leslie Thompson, he was another one — and Len Dare. And my poor old mother. She was a good woman, she worked hard on the droving track. Right up to the last she was working on a station. She fell sick one day, the flying doctor brought her in to hospital, and she died the next day. And Dad — he tried to teach me right, too. I'd like to mention two other fellas I still know today, as well. Ronnie Finlay and Snowy Edwards. They was part of my learning and growing up.

"When I recall how them old people worked years ago, there's no comparison with today. There are too many machines today — I preferred the old times, even though some of the conditions was bad.

"But there was prejudice and racism everywhere then, and now I think everyone is learning to become more tolerant to others. I feel that in the outback — I don't say in the city — people are becoming more understanding of one another. You know, white people never understood us before because they never learned about us. That's the big failure of the past. We had to go their way and they never gave us a chance to show them the things we knew about the country. — All right, we learned how to become as good stockmen as them, but that wasn't enough. It shoulda gone both ways."

"You don't believe times are better now, Jack?"

"No, they're worse in some ways, in spite of the better understanding I was speaking of. But there's not nearly enough discipline of the kids, and the respect for our elders which we used to have when we were kids seems to have gone by the board. There's too much justice in some areas, and no justice in others — it all seems too weak.

"If you want to get anywhere in life you got to get off your butt and do something. You got to try and make it yourself, not give up halfway." He paused. "I believe that Christ died for us. That belief was handed down by my mother, and it was handed down to her. I believe Christ died for all of us. He saved me in my time of crisis and kept me for a purpose. Some of the experiences I've had to cope with in my life have helped me to communicate with people today in similar situations. If people want to listen, I'll sit down and talk to them."

Jack Guttie has seen much in his life. He has seen the mysterious Min-Min light that bobs and weaves its erratic course on inland nights. He has been visited by the apparitions of lost loved ones watching over him in his hour of need. He has witnessed strange happenings at Yulabertie waterhole, the largest and deepest waterhole on Coopers Creek, where cattle and people have inexplicably disappeared. He has heard the Dreamtime stories of the spirit that inhabits that waterhole, a legend common among many outback tribes and related to the life-giving waters of the inland. And he has never forgotten the strange inheritance his mother told him about when he was a boy and she showed him his birthplace. "You're not old or wise enough to have it yet," she told him, "but it will be yours when you grow up." Possibly that inheritance is related to the many strange tales I have heard concerning Aboriginal treasure in that part of Australia. I have written of this elsewhere in this book. Or it could be knowledge and wisdom, the greatest treasures of all.

Jack has had a fulfilling past, and his future holds exciting promise, with a new bride to share with him the hoped-for riches of the opal mine he discovered while mustering in 1948, and a visit to his birthplace to search for that mysterious inheritance.

For this one-time drover, station hand, windmill expert, railway worker, counsellor and language teacher, who was born under a coolabah tree on Coopers Creek, the best things in life could be yet to come.

Also by Herb Wharton

Unbranded

From the riotous picnic races to the famous Mt Isa rodeo, from childhood in the yumba to gutsy outback pubs, Unbranded presents a strikingly original vision of Australia.

With a rollicking cast of stockmen, shearers, barmaids and tourists, this novel is the story of three men. Sandy is a white man; Bindi, a Murri; Mulga is related on his mother's side to Bindi, and on his Irish father's side to Sandy. Their saga — and enduring friendship — covers forty years in the mulga country of the far west. It tells how Sandy achieves his dream of owning a cattle empire; how Bindi regains part of his tribal lands for his people; and how Mulga finally sits down to write about their shared experiences. Mulga's journey also brings him face-to-face with the dark side of urban despair and his people's struggle with alcohol.

ISBN 0 7022 2444 8

University of Queensland
Press —

Rosanne Fitzgibbons

Sue Abbey
     or

~~3377 H~~
3365 1111